ACTING FOR A LIVING

ACTING
FOR A LIVING

How to Act *Outside* Hollywood

Become an Actor / Work in Film, TV & Video / Make it Your Career

ROY MCCREREY

ISBN: 978-1466383401

Editor: Andrea Barbian
Cover and interior design: Rosamond Grupp

www.actingforaliving.com

For My Parents,

James and Valerie McCrerey

ABOUT THE AUTHOR

To date, Roy McCrerey has been cast in eight feature films (*The Patriot; One Missed Call, The Joneses*), nine television series (*One Tree Hill; Drop Dead Diva; Necessary Roughness*), and scores of national, network and regional commercials. He has hosted programs for *PBS, CNN, Turner Broadcasting* and *HGTV*, as well as many of America's top Fortune 500 corporations, including *Microsoft, IBM, Coca Cola, Home Depot* and *Walmart*. In terms of annual earnings, he has been among the top 2% of professional actors in the U.S.A. for 19 consecutive years.

CONTENTS

My Story

"Every exit is an entry somewhere."
- Tom Stoppard

If you could be anything you want to be tomorrow, what would you be? Think hard before you answer. A girl asked me that question once and it changed my entire life.

We were talking on the phone at the time, and I remember feeling so drained and exhausted that I could barely hold the receiver up to my ear. I was wearing my best suit and tie, and lying flat on my back on the living room floor. I was having a bad day.

It had started out well-enough. That morning, I had bounced out of bed, showered, shaved and inhaled a quick breakfast. I had avoided most of the traffic and arrived at work early, only to find the front door locked and a crude sign taped to the window. It read, *"Out of Business"*.

It was 1991. I was twenty-six years old and my life was a shambles. I had no job, no girlfriend, and no prospects of either appearing anytime soon. I was broke, depressed, and up to my eyeballs in debt. I had been a complete failure at everything I had tried. And I had tried *everything*.

In a series of minor catastrophes, I had attempted to sell real estate, life insurance, automobiles (both new and used), water conditioners for the home, mailing and shipping equipment for the office, and fraternity and sorority sportswear to colleges and universities around the country.

I had worked for the Better Business Bureau (for one week), trained to be a private detective (for one day), and filled-in as a substitute teacher. I'd tried my hand at waiting tables, bartending and oyster-shucking and found that I despised all three. At one point, I even resorted to selling vacuum cleaners door-to-door for a long, loathsome summer. I never sold a single unit.

Now, staring forlornly up at my ceiling fan, it occurred to me that I had reached the lowest point of all. The cruel irony was that it had come just as I had begun to make a little headway.

Six months before, I had been hired as a sales manager. Unlike all of my previous professions, this was a salaried position in a solid, nine-to-five job. It came with health insurance and a bonus plan. The company had even agreed to take over my car payments. At last, it seemed as if things were turning around. I had paid my dues, and was ready to reap the rewards. The future looked bright. I was an executive.

Then, just as I was about to plant my flag in the corporate summit, it all came tumbling down. In an instant, I was at rock-bottom again. I'm sure I must have looked quite pitiful lying motionless on the floor of my apartment; a broken Humpty Dumpty.

Anne, a former co-worker, was on the other end of the line trying to cheer me up. It wasn't working.

What could she say? There was no avoiding the fact that my outlook was bleak. I couldn't think of a single reason to get up off the floor. I was resigning myself to the thought of spending the rest of my life next to a coffee table, when she asked the ultimate question:

"If you could be anything you want to be *tomorrow*, what would you be?"

"I don't know," I muttered.

"Think about it. You can be anything…anything at all. What pops into your mind?" I took a deep breath and let out a long, heavy sigh. "An actor, I guess…"

It was the first thing that came out of my mouth, and to this day, I don't know why I said it. In college, I had double-majored in political science and economics. Acting was the farthest thing from my mind. In my entire life, I had only taken part in one theatrical production, and that anxious and somewhat traumatic experience had taken place in the second grade. I was a duck.

"How the hell am I going to be an actor, Anne? I don't know the first thing about it. Who makes a living as an actor, anyway?"

"Well, it's funny that you should ask me that because, believe it or not, I just met an actor a couple of days ago. He's a friend of a friend of mine. Maybe you should give him a call and ask him how he does it?" Anne had lots of friends, along with an almost infinite supply of patience.

"A friend of a friend of yours? Are you serious? And he makes a living as an actor?"

"Yup, apparently so. He's had quite a few speaking roles in movies, too. Give him a call. What have you got to lose? You never know; you might try it out and hate it, or you could be looking back 10 years from now and saying: Wow – look where I started, and look where I am now."

Anne was right. And somewhere deep down in my jaded psyche, I knew it. Gradually, I began to warm up to the idea.

After all, what *did* I have to lose? It wasn't as if things could get much worse. Ever since graduation, I'd been putting all my energy into jobs I hated, simply to make a buck. In the end, the results had always been the same; I wound-up miserable and broke. Maybe it was time for a new approach? Instead of focusing on money, perhaps I should focus on something that interested me, instead?

And that was all it took. It was nothing more than a quick mental decision to spend my life doing what I *wanted* to do, rather than struggling along like some hamster on a wheel in the hope that a pot of gold at the end of it all would justify my misery. A few minutes earlier, I had lacked the strength to lift my head off the floor. Now I was up on my feet and pacing around the room like a tiger.

I thanked Anne, hung up the phone, and immediately began to set a plan of action in motion. Looking back now, I can honestly say that it was the turning point of my life.

WHY YOU NEED THIS BOOK

"You have to understand the rules of the game. And then you have to play better than anyone else."
- Albert Einstein

No matter where I am or whom I happen to be talking to, as soon as I mention that I am an actor the reaction is nearly always the same: "Really? Are you serious? What sort of acting do you do? Do you do it full-time? How did you get started?"

It seems the world of the professional actor is both fascinating and mysterious to almost everyone on the planet. Indeed, many are surprised to hear that such a career is even possible. Want a good laugh? Just try telling a guidance counselor or job-recruiter that you are seriously considering acting as a full-time profession. Watch their facial expression.

It is as if the key to a successful acting career is a closely guarded secret, passed down from generation to generation. This image is further enhanced when we consider how many movie stars have relatives in the business. All indications seem to point to an industry mired in nepotism, but I really don't think it's that simple. That's because, like all businesses, showbiz is irrevocably bound to a financial "bottom line". These days, even the low-budget Hollywood movies are big money affairs and putting together the funding for them is never an easy thing.

You might think major Hollywood stars have more than enough wealth to make any film they choose, but that is far from the truth. In fact, there are only a handful of individuals in Hollywood – perhaps no more than half a dozen, with enough power and money to make a movie with no outside help. And even though these lucky few have the resources to pull it off, they won't. Movie-making is an expensive, risky business; and smart investors will always try to limit their risk.

At this very moment, you can be sure that there are scores of major film stars pushing their own projects forward; searching for investors to bankroll a screenplay they love. Most of these actors are envisioning a film that could take their career to the next level, but not one of them will contribute so much as a single dollar of their own money in order to help finance their project. Why not? Because bankrolling movies is a big-time roll of the dice. In order to risk your money on a movie you have to be either crazy rich or just plain crazy. Believe it or not, the majority of Hollywood movie stars are neither.

Which brings us back to the issue of nepotism. In reality, when the time comes to hire an actor, whoever their mom or pop happens to be is largely irrelevant. The days of handing someone a lead role in a movie just because they are the niece of a good golfing buddy are long gone. There is too much money at stake, too many hands in the pot and too many asses on the line for personal favors anymore. If you want a part in a movie (even a measly, one-line role), you are going to have to prove you're the right person for the job. You are going to have to earn it.

Are there exceptions? You bet; but not to any significant degree. Nepotism *does* exist in Hollywood; it's just not the driving career-force that many assume. Personally, I think what is often mistaken as nepotism is really nothing more than good, sound advice. Having access to a family member who understands how this business works provides an actor with an enormous advantage. All other things being equal, anyone who can get solid advice early in their career is going to have a head start over their competition. That edge can make all the difference in the world.

Again, professional acting is a mystery to nearly everyone. Most actors will spend the better part of their careers just trying to figure out how this game works, without ever getting an opportunity to play it. By the time they figure it out (assuming they ever do) their best hope is to pass along their hard-earned knowledge to their children.

I don't have any kids, so I'm passing my knowledge on to you. Much of what I have learned over the past twenty years has been the result of trial and error. Some of it has been observation and intuition, and a fair amount of it has been pure, dumb, luck. Throughout my career, I have done my best to learn from my mistakes and successes, as well as those of others.

Acting advice is not hard to come by. A quick web search will reveal a wide array of forums and message boards crammed with all sorts of opinions about how one should go about pursuing a career. The problem is that much of this advice comes from people with little or no professional acting experience. Don't get me wrong: It's a free country and everybody has a right to their opinion. I'm just saying that an uninformed opinion can do you more harm than good.

Finding experienced actors who are willing to help you out can be a little tricky. Where do you begin? Who should you trust?

As soon as I decided to embark upon an acting career, I began reading lots of books. I found the autobiographies of celebrities to be inspirational and entertaining, but of little practical use to me. There was no definable pattern of success that I could emulate. Their lives were all so different and their backgrounds so diverse that it was difficult to see how I could apply their unique circumstances to my own career.

Of course, there were plenty of books in print about acting, but successful actors wrote almost none of them. Most of the authors seemed to be casting directors or talent agents. Why not actors? Many acting books tended to focus on technique, which was something I could learn in a classroom. I wanted to know how to go about developing and maintaining a career. I had so many questions...

Should I start out in local theatre, or would it be better to move to Hollywood immediately? Perhaps it would be easier to break into the business in New York? Was drama school worth the investment? If so, which one should I choose? Maybe it made more sense to save my money and take weekend workshops or ongoing classes? But how could I be sure my instructors were competent and teaching me the right things? When and how should I approach talent agents? And perhaps, the most important question of all: Did I have a realistic chance of making it as an actor, or was I just kidding myself and wasting my time?

This then, is the book that I wish I could have found. In it, I address all of these questions in detail, as well as scores of other issues vital to anyone considering a professional acting career. It is my hope that after reading it, you will not only have a clear understanding of the rules of this particular game, but the knowledge required to play at a consistently high level. I wish you the best of success.

SUCCESS

"Choose a career you love, and you will never have to work a day in your life."
- Confucius

Before you can reasonably determine your chance of becoming a successful actor, it might be a good idea to consider how you define success. I thought about this a lot when I first started out in the business. What were my goals? What could I reasonably expect to achieve?

There's no question that fame and fortune sounded appealing. Like most young actors, I imagined what it would be like to pick up my first Oscar. You've got to give a shout out to Mum and Dad, obviously, but should I thank them before or after the director? I could easily picture myself with a Ferrari and a couple of super-models. There would be late night talk-show appearances, a private jet and parties at the Playboy Mansion. Not bad…not bad at all.

Even in my wildest moments of delusion, however, I knew that the odds of any of those things actually happening were pretty remote. And yet, *someone* has to be the best actor every year. Why not me?

That's one of the great things about this business; the sky truly is the limit. Once you get going, there's no telling where you'll wind up. That sort of unlimited potential had been sorely missing in my earlier career choices. The realization that almost anything was possible gave me the energy to jump up out of bed each morning. Life is a whole lot more interesting when you enjoy what you're doing,

I decided that the changes in my attitude were so positive that I had little choice but to pursue acting, regardless of where it led me. The issue of fame soon became irrelevant. Acting was the one profession that could hold my interest. It was the only job that seemed worth doing.

Today, I have what can only be described as a dream career. I work, on average, about two days per week. This schedule varies greatly, as you might imagine. There are some weeks when I work every day and others when I don't work at all. Nevertheless, the overall workload has remained remarkably consistent over the past two decades.

Also, the amount of hours in a "workday" is never the same. It can last as long as 10 or 12 hours (I get massive overtime for anything over 8 hours) or it can be as short as 30 minutes. No, that is not a misprint…30 minutes! And when you tally up the total number of hours that I work on average, the pay that I receive borders on the obscene.

According to the U.S. Gov. Bureau of Labor Statistics, the median salary for a heart surgeon in the United States is currently $105.66 per hour. Top surgeons (those in the upper 10%) earn an average of $200 per hour. My day rate for an industrial narration job is $1500 ($187.50 per hour if we shoot for the full eight hours). For commercials, television and film, it averages out to be far more than that due to residuals. Occasionally, I am paid *thousands* of dollars per hour; and I never had to struggle through medical school. I don't have to worry about dealing with any blood, stress, or malpractice insurance either.

In fact, my "work" isn't really work at all. Just like professional athletes, I am paid to play. I often have a chance to interact with the some of the finest talent, directors, producers, crew members and ad agents in the business. Almost without exception, these people are creative, fun, intelligent and a real pleasure to be around. When I am working on the set with movie stars, I'm acknowledged as a peer. Unlike extras or autograph hounds – I am recognized as a fellow "artist", and treated as such by everyone on the set. I am given my own trailer (smaller than the stars, but mine nonetheless) and I am pampered and waited on, almost to the point of absurdity. It's really quite nice, actually.

As far as benefits are concerned – I have excellent health insurance and retirement through the Screen Actors Guild. I'm also a member of the SAG Credit union. Any member of SAG can join the credit union and I highly recommend that you do. Once you're in, you're a member for life. It's a terrific organization which has consistently quoted me outstanding rates on both car and mortgage loans.

One of the things that made me most apprehensive about pursuing acting was the issue of job security. It worried a lot of my friends and family too (When my brother-in-law heard I wanted to be an actor, he was convinced I'd lost my mind).

As it turned out, job security has been a non-factor. Indeed, I have never had such fabulous job security in all my life! Technically speaking, it's impossible for me to be laid off, since I don't work for anybody. And so long as television, movies, radio, businesses and corporations of every shape and size exist, there will be a demand for the services I provide. In a world where more people than ever are scrambling to be informed and entertained, that is about as secure as anyone can ever hope to be.

But of all the wonderful perks about full-time acting, the best thing about it is the freedom that it gives me. I answer to no one. Having slaved under some real losers in the past, it's impossible to put a price-tag on the value of independence. There is nothing like the sense of well-being that successful self-employment provides. Simply not having a boss is worth many tens of thousands of dollars a year to me.

On the days when I have a booking – I am happy to have a job where I will be well compensated. On the days when I don't have a booking – I am happy to have the day off to spend and enjoy as I please. It is the best of all possible worlds.

When you have an average of five days off per week, you tend to have plenty of free time on your hands, so I naturally have a lot of hobbies and interests. Lately, I've been spending most of my time writing. I'm also doing some comedy improv and I plan to start taking photography lessons soon. On rainy days, if I feel like watching an old movie, reading a good book, or taking a nap – I do it. If I feel like flying off to Europe for three weeks, I do that. I have enough money to live my life as I please and plenty of free time in which to enjoy it. Does that sound like a successful career to you?

I am no De Niro or Pacino, and I never will be. On the other hand, I can hardly consider myself to be a failure, either. Acting has provided me with an income and lifestyle that I could scarcely have imagined in my younger years. It has quite literally turned out to be a million-dollar-career, and I am amazed to think that I fell into it almost entirely by chance. That's not to say my life is perfect. I have my own share of problems and issues just like anybody else. But as far as I'm concerned, a successful acting career doesn't have to revolve around Oscars and Emmys.

Perhaps you have a different concept of success? Maybe your goal is to become a famous movie star and you're unwilling to settle for anything less. Fair enough; if you're going to dream, you might as well dream big. However, I would caution you to keep at least one foot on the ground at all times. No matter how you slice it, the chances that you will become famous in this business are remote. Just how remote depends upon many factors, but even if you are fortunate enough to possess top-level talent and drop-dead-gorgeous looks, your odds of achieving stardom are something akin to your chances of winning the lottery. Actually, that might be overstating the matter. After all, someone wins the lottery every day, but only a handful of people become movie stars each year. I am not saying it can't happen for you; I'm just saying I wouldn't bet the farm on it, that's all.

If you are bound and determined to head for Hollywood and take your shot at the big time, I'll provide you with a game plan for success towards the end of this book. I can't promise that you'll ever make it, but I can assure you that if you follow my advice, your chances will improve considerably.

In the end, the question you have to ask yourself is the same that any would-be professional athlete, musician or artist has to ask himself or herself: "Do I have what it takes? "If you think that you do, then go for it. You have nothing to lose. Even if it doesn't work out, at least you can say you gave it a shot. Failure isn't difficult to live with; not trying is.

WHAT DOES IT TAKE?

*"Laurence [Olivier] used to say that an actor must have
the body of a god, and a voice equal to the full range
and power of an orchestra. Incredibly, even into his later
years – he actually had both of those things."*

- Ian Holm

*"For an actress to be a success, she must have the face
of Venus, the brains of Minerva, the grace of Terpsichore,
the memory of Macaulay, the figure of Juno, and the hide
of a rhinoceros."*

- Ethel Barrymore

Everybody knows that in order to be a doctor you have to be smart
enough to make it through medical school. If you want to be a life-
guard, you are going to have to be an excellent swimmer. If you ever
expect to make it as an NFL linebacker, you had better be big, strong
and fast. The qualifications for most jobs are not a mystery, but opinions vary widely as to what it takes to become an actor.

Some say you need "stage presence", while others insist that it
comes down to "God-given talent". Somewhat frustratingly (in my
experience, at least), the people who use these terms are rarely able to
go into further specifics and explain what they actually mean by them.

That isn't very helpful to us. You cannot assess your chances fairly using abstract terminology.

So what's the answer? Maybe acting doesn't take any real skill at all? Certainly there are those who believe that to be the case. There are undoubtedly famous people on television who seem to have no obvious talent. Not understanding what makes them so special, it's easy to jump to the conclusion that anyone can become an actor. Maybe it is all a matter of who you know (or who you sleep with), and being in the right place at the right time?

It is because of this sort of reasoning that many people spend years of their lives waiting to be discovered. It's as if they expect Steven Spielberg to spot them in a grocery store one day, drop everything, and come sprinting over to offer them a part in his next motion picture. There are tens of thousands in Los Angeles right now who are waiting for this to happen. We'll go into more detail about that in the next chapter, but for now, it's enough that you understand that such thinking is madness. These are the people whom we do not want to emulate under any circumstances.

In my opinion, there is a skill set required for acting, and there is nothing mysterious or abstract about it. The most important criteria for an actor are *reading*, *speaking* and *imagination*. These are the three pillars on which the future of your career will depend. A fourth factor is *self-confidence*, but that comes as a result of experience and success. If you read well, speak well and have a good imagination, I'm willing to go out on a limb right now and say that you almost certainly have what it takes to be a good actor. Even if you never make it to the "big time", it is safe to say that if you are interested in this business, it is probably going to be worth your while to pursue it.

If you feel that you are deficient in any of these areas (or even in all three), that doesn't necessarily mean that you have no chance. It is still possible that you could make it happen. However, you should understand that you will be starting off on the back foot, and that you will have to make up a considerable amount of ground in order to catch up with the pack. That's going to take time and effort on your part. You will to have to work hard to overcome those deficiencies.

Fortunately, I happen to know of a way in which you can kill three birds with one stone. Believe it or not, it is possible to develop your reading, speaking and imagination with a single, simple exercise. You can do it in as little as 30 minutes a day. What's more, it's actually a lot of fun. Interested?

It's simple; all you have to do is *read*. Read books; and read them every day. Books force you to activate your imagination in a way that few other things can. As you read, your brain has to process all sorts of information. It has no choice but to create mental images of the people and places that you're reading about in order for you to follow along with the story. It sounds simple (and it is), but reading puts your imagination to work, big-time. Your mind doesn't get anything like that sort of exercise when you kick back and watch TV. Reading is not only relaxing and entertaining; it is a workout for your brain.

It also helps to improve your speech – even if you only read silent-ly to yourself. That's because your mind becomes more accustomed to language as it learns to comprehend and process words more easily. In the same way hand-eye coordination is important to most athletes, "mouth-eye" coordination is vital to an actor. You should be able to read out loud effortlessly, and in your own natural voice. Ultimately, you should be able to read so fluidly and easily that anyone listening to you on the phone or in an adjoining room would be unable to tell that you are reading at all. Instead, it should sound as though you are talking to someone. That takes practice. The more you read, the easier it becomes.

If you read aloud, your diction will also improve. In fact, it will improve even if you read silently (though at a slower pace). As an ac-tor, the more articulate you are, the more successful you will be. If we can't understand you, you're not going to go very far in this business. You don't have to have a booming voice and sound like a game show host or a radio announcer from the 1940's, but you do need to be clear. If you have a speech impediment, don't let it deter you; many actors and orators have overcome them. A thick accent isn't necessarily a deal-breaker, either. Sometimes it can even work to your advantage. However, unless you can drop it when you need to, an unusual accent will severely limit the roles you're able to play.

There are other benefits to reading, as well. For example: It's an actor's job to be able to see things from another person's point of view. That's a lot easier to do when you're intelligent and open-minded. As it happens, reading promotes both. It also helps build a strong self-esteem, which is vital to an actor. Having your work critiqued is part of this job. If you're insecure, you're going to have a tough time dealing with the direction and criticism that you will inevitably hear from time to time. A healthy self-esteem will also enable you to remain objective about your own abilities. Self-deception is one of the greatest dangers in this business.

I can't think of any activity that gives you more real-world benefits than reading. It has been estimated that it is the single greatest indicator of a child's future success. I can assure you, that is doubly true if you intend to be an actor. You should make it a habit to read every day; even if only for a few minutes in bed before turning out the light. Think of it as a daily workout for your brain. Everyone knows that the human body needs regular exercise in order to stay in shape. Your mind is no different.

What else does an actor need? Well, an engaging personality is a big plus. You don't have to be a stand-up comic, or take over a room every time you walk in, but successful actors are nearly always charming when you meet them. You should find it relatively easy to make a good first impression. Auditions are a key element of this business and an audition really isn't much more than a job interview. If you're the sort of person who performs well in interview situations, that's a very good sign. It bodes well for your acting career.

As far as physical requirements are concerned, being healthy and attractive certainly doesn't hurt. Actors who look healthy tend to work more than those who don't. This isn't always the case, but generally speaking, it's true.

While it is almost impossible to be too healthy, an actor who is too beautiful runs the risk of being labeled as a "model-type" (i.e.: too perfect to be real). That can be a problem, because many people tend to assume that stunningly beautiful people can't act. This is nonsense, of course. In reality, there is no correlation whatsoever between a person's physical appearance and their acting ability. One has nothing to do with the other.

The truth is that your looks will probably be less of an issue than you imagine. Think about all the actors who have enjoyed fabulous careers despite being relatively "average" looking – or even downright ugly. There are roles for every shape, size, color and age in this business. It's how comfortable you are with your appearance that truly matters.

There is one more factor which is rarely, if ever, addressed. That's somewhat surprising when you consider nearly all the top actors have it, and the majority of unsuccessful actors don't. It is with this "missing ingredient" that much of this book will be concerned. What I'm referring to is *attitude*. Not attitude in the sense that it might be used to describe a diva or prima donna, but rather in the sense of having the right mindset. If you don't have the proper mental approach, you're not going to make it into the upper echelons of this industry. It is that simple.

Many people can act. There are thousands of actors who, by all appearances, seem to have everything necessary for success at the highest levels. They look good, speak well and are loaded with talent. They just can't seem to make it happen. The problem for so many of these people is simply their attitude. It isn't that it's *bad* – just that it's *wrong*. If they could only get their minds turned in the right direction, their careers would receive a much-needed shot of adrenaline. How so? Well, that's what we're going to talk about in the next chapter.

Bonus Round:

Take a trip to your local library or bookstore and pick out a book. I know, you're already reading this one – and I am grateful, but for our purposes this book doesn't count. I want you to choose a work of fiction. The genre is completely up to you: Classical literature, western, horror, sci-fi, fantasy, romance, crime drama – I don't care what it is, just as long as it's fiction and you find it interesting. Your assignment is to spend at least 30 minutes per day reading this book. If you lose interest in it, fine. Go and get another one. Keep looking until you come across one that you can't put down. It's out there somewhere.

If you have kids and find it tough to get thirty minutes of quiet time alone to yourself, then choose something your children will enjoy and read it to them. They'll love it. Not only is it a perfect way to spend quality time with them, it will give you a nice linguist workout to boot.

Make "reading time" part of your daily routine and it will soon become one of the highlights of your day. What's more – it will make you a better actor.

THE MAJORITY IS WRONG

"Whenever you find yourself on the side of the majority, it is time to pause and reflect."

- Mark Twain

"Hollywood is still the Mecca for good or bad, but it isn't the beginning or end for filmmaking."

- Robert Duvall

Most Americans assume that if you want to make a living as an actor, you have no choice but to live and work in either New York City or Los Angeles. This assumption has been so widely held for so long that it's now considered a straightforward fact and beyond any debate. It's what all the acting books say, it's what industry "insiders" will tell you and it is certainly what the vast majority of wannabe actors believe.

The majority is wrong.

In 2010, the Screen Actors' Guild released figures showing that 95% of its members earned less than $7000 for the year. That is a truly shocking statistic; especially when you consider the majority of these people live in either Los Angeles or New York; two of the most expensive cities in the United States. You have to wonder how they manage to survive. Clearly, the majority is doing something wrong.

Now, before you get too discouraged about what essentially amounts to a 95% failure rate for actors, let me just take a moment to give you some reassurance. Things are not quite as bad as they might seem. If we're smart about it, we can not only beat those odds, but use them to our advantage. For starters, the fact that most of the millions of struggling actors reside in two cities is good for our purposes. At least we know where they are and how to avoid them. This is why I'm advising you to stay away from New York and Los Angeles completely – at least early in your career. By avoiding those two cities, you eliminate the vast majority of your competition right off the bat. Regardless of whether you reside in or near Atlanta, Boston, Chicago, Denver, Dallas, Miami, New Orleans, Orlando, Pittsburgh, Seattle, Washington D.C., or any other major metropolitan area – the competition you will face as an actor will be *miniscule* compared to what you will be up against in New York and L.A.

Of course, there is less work in the regional markets, but that fact is more than offset by the reduction in competition. Furthermore, many of the actors in the regional markets lack the basic skills necessary to compete on a professional level. That may sound harsh, but it is a fact. The majority of regional actors are part-timers. Acting is a fun way for them to supplement their income. Most have a "real job", which they rely on to pay the bills.

Taking all professional actors into account on a nationwide basis, you will probably need to break into the top 2% in order to earn a solid, consistent income. This is just an estimate, of course. There is no precise way to know how many actors we are dealing with since many who consider themselves professionals are not in the unions. In any event, it's safe to say there are a lot of them.

However, once we move away from the bright lights of New York and Hollywood and eliminate those cities from our calculations altogether, the numbers start to become much more reasonable. In the regional markets, 20% of the actors will do 80% of the work. The middle 60% fight over the leftovers, and the bottom 20% never work at all. While these figures are again approximations, they closely reflect conversations I have had with talent agents in various markets around the country.

Although exact numbers are impossible to calculate, there's no question that your odds of making a full-time living as an actor dramatically increase outside New York and Los Angeles. Regardless of where you live, as long as you are talented and marketable, the number of actors who will be direct, legitimate competitors of yours should be relatively small. Depending on the location, we might be talking about no more than 5 to 10 individuals; possibly less. Those are manageable odds, and certainly far better than what you would be up against in the major markets, where your competition would be numbered in the hundreds or thousands.

In the regional markets, you are still going to have to be among the top 20% in order to thrive, but that's true of any sales industry and most professions today. If you have a skill set for acting (reading, speaking, imagination) and the desire to succeed, breaking into the top 20% shouldn't be all that difficult for you. And this is before we even begin to take into consideration any special qualities, skills or other factors that might give you an advantage over your competition.

We already know that 95% of SAG members earn less than $7,000 per year. Depressing? You bet. It's tough to pay the bills in this day and age on that sort of an income. You don't have to be a math whiz to see that what the majority of actors are doing isn't exactly paying off for them. Despite the high profile of the Screen Actors' Guild, the truth is that the overwhelming majority of SAG actors don't earn enough money in their chosen profession to support themselves, much less a family.

Instead, the majority of SAG actors survive by working "real jobs", and picking up acting gigs whenever good fortune strikes, the planets align, or they just happen to get lucky. Why do they live like this? Because they're under the impression that that is how the acting business works. You have to put your dues in. You have to struggle along as a starving actor living on tuna fish, peanut butter, and macaroni and cheese – until one day your ship comes in and you're "discovered". The rest, as they say, is history. It's a rags-to-riches story with an almost fairytale quality about it – and there's a good reason for that: *It is a fairytale.*

Actors have been "discovered" in the past, but it's a much rarer occurrence than most people realize. And it is becoming rarer every year. The odds that a big-shot director will spot your face across the room and offer you the world (with no strings attached) are not even worth calculating. They are certainly not enough for you to base your career on. Contrast the handful of success stories you may have heard with the untold *millions* who have struggled to make it in Hollywood over the past hundred years, and you will begin to see the absurdity of the situation. Faced with such long odds, only the most optimistic (or deluded) dreamer would waste their life pursuing such a plan; which, I suppose, goes a long way to explaining why Los Angeles is so full of optimistic and deluded dreamers. It isn't that these folks aren't talented – many of them are. It's simply a question of math. There aren't enough roles to go around.

Not all Hollywood actors are wasting their time, of course. Some have agents and managers and are working consistently. They are auditioning for roles on movies and television shows all the time. These are the individuals who have their act together. They are "in the game" and they are playing to win. However, they are in a tiny minority.

Most Hollywood actors do not have an agent or a manager, and they rarely get a chance to audition for anything. Instead, they spend their time and money on acting classes (which may or may not be helping) and obsessing over their physical appearance. Then they hang out at the beach, night-clubs or parties hoping to meet somebody with connections who will set them on the path to fame and fortune. They are waiting for an invitation to a party that is never going to arrive.

Successful actors aren't *discovered*; they are *developed*. Even though you may have never heard of a hot new actor before, that doesn't mean they've just sprung up out of the ground. Behind every star that seems to suddenly appear out of nowhere is a proven track record of success. It may have come from a theatrical background, an obscure film, a foreign television show, a hit record, a popular commercial, a standup comedy routine or a series of truly mesmerizing auditions – but I can assure you that it is there. *It has to be there.* These days, there is just too much money at stake for it not to be.

Many struggling, wannabe actors could easily turn themselves into successful, full-time actors if they would take the time to learn how this business really works. This would allow them to approach their careers in a realistic manner and give them a fighting chance of working consistently.

Instead, most will continue to follow their dream (or to be more accurate, fantasy) for decades, before eventually giving up and drifting off into some other profession. This usually means starting over in middle age with little or no money. Believe it or not, I know actors who have spent 20 years or more trying to make it in Hollywood, only to reach their mid-40's without any savings or health insurance – much less a retirement plan. Don't let that happen to you.

I'm not saying you shouldn't follow your dream. On the contrary, you *should* follow it. Just take care that you follow it wisely. Self-delusion can be a very painful and expensive lesson. It can rob you of some of the best years of your life.

I have lived and worked in Hollywood and have many friends who still continue to live and work there. I'm going to tell you the same thing that I tell each and every one of them: In my opinion, Los Angeles is absolute worst place on Earth for you to pursue an acting career.

There are only a few exceptions to this otherwise hard and fast rule:

1. Talented and attractive actors (especially minority actors) who are already SAG members and are under the age of 25. The younger you are, the better your chances.

2. Talented actors who have recently graduated from a nationally-renowned dramatic institution.

3. Accomplished stand-up comedians, musicians or singers.

4. Highly unusual physical types (e.g.: Danny DeVito, Richard Kiel, Vern Troyer, etc…)

5. Actors who have booked a major role in at least one film or TV show. Obviously, the bigger the role and project, the better.

If you don't meet one or more of the above criteria, you're better off staying out of L.A. As a rule of thumb; if Hollywood isn't calling, don't bother knocking. Consider yourself warned.

True story: When I first moved to L.A. in the 1990's, I signed with the Tisherman Agency. My agent was the colorful Malcolm Cassel. Malcolm started out as a child actor and has continued to live and work in Hollywood ever since. During our initial interview, I happened to mention that I was originally from England and could do a lot of authentic British accents. Malcolm just stared blankly at me for a moment…then sighed.

"Roy", he said, "This is *Tinsel Town*. This is the largest collection of talent on planet Earth. If a director calls me up tomorrow and says, "Malcolm, I need a one-legged, Hungarian fire-juggler," my response to him is going to be, 'Which province? – 'cause I got him."

It was an early wake-up call.

Hollywood doesn't need people with special skills. In fact they don't need any more actors – talented, beautiful or otherwise. They're already swimming in them. Tell someone you are an actor in Seattle and they will say "Wow, that is so cool." Tell someone you are an actor in L.A. and they will roll their eyes and walk away like you asked them for bus money. That's not an exaggeration. Hollywood needs actors like a cruise ship needs rats.

Again, I am not saying this to depress you, I'm just trying to bring you up to speed with the harsh reality of the situation. This is your life and whether or not you realize it, time is your most precious asset. If I were you, I wouldn't waste one second of my life knocking on the doors of Hollywood agents like some encyclopedia salesman. You want the big shots in Hollywood to notice you? Fine. Then you need to make *them* come to *you*. That may not be all that easy to do, but believe me, it's a heck of a lot easier than trying to do it the other way around.

We will talk more about that later. For now, forget about Hollywood. And while you're at it, forget about New York City, too. The truth is you don't need either one of them in order to have a successful acting career. Not while there's so much money to be made in the regional markets.

What do I mean by regional markets? Basically, regional markets (or regionals) refers to any major city in the world *other* than New York City or Los Angeles.

Over the past two decades, a variety of factors have combined to blow regional markets wide open and turn them into viable places for an actor to live and work. These factors include:

- A tax-credit war for Hollywood's business
- The rise of independent films and HD cameras
- The growth of cable television
- The emergence of the internet

Another factor would be the development of high speed cable lines, which has had a major impact in the voice over industry. Because of ultra-clear cable lines and ISDN, it is now possible for voice over artists to record live sessions with a studio from anywhere in the world.

With the rising costs of movie production, producers are constantly on the lookout for cheaper locations in which to shoot their films. Throughout the 1990's, Canada was the place to be. The tax incentives offered were just too good for Hollywood to pass up. Towards the latter part of the decade, some American states started getting into the act in a big way, and the result has been a tax incentive war for the movie industry's business.

Each year, U.S. states and foreign countries are passing newer and ever more attractive tax laws in an effort to lure movies and television shows to their doorsteps. That's great news for regional actors, because the incentives usually stipulate that local actors must be employed in order for the film's production to qualify for the state tax credits. Even when those stipulations don't exist, local actors are often given preference in casting, because they save the production from having to pay housing and transportation costs.

Last summer I had a chance to attend the sold-out *Locations Trade Show* in Santa Monica, CA., where over 300 exhibitors from more than 30 countries spanning six continents were in attendance. Each booth was full of representatives touting their particular state/country/ region's tax incentives. It was incredible. The world is in smoking-hot competition for the film industry's business, and Hollywood is listening. Over 3400 Hollywood studios, producers and production company executives showed up over a three day period.

Now, Europe is getting into the act with the *Seville International Location Expo*, in Seville, Spain. This represents Europe's first locations trade fair in which audiovisual producers and directors will meet with exhibitors promoting their locations for feature films, short films, videos, advertisements, etc… Which simply means more work for regional actors all over the world.

Independent films are another source of income and experience for regional actors. With hi-definition digital cameras available at reasonable prices, it's becoming more and more viable to shoot low-budget movies. In fact, the most profitable movie in motion picture history was an independent film that was shot in the woods of northern Georgia. *"The Blair Witch Project"*, cost $35,000 to produce, and grossed $140 million at the box office. Not too shabby.

Cable has been another boon; providing a means for smaller businesses to advertise on television. Local and regional commercials may look cheap, but they are a great way for beginning actors to rack up some valuable experience and income. As we shall soon see, it's also possible to negotiate some rather respectable paychecks.

Cable and satellite television have spawned countless shows on a wide range of channels. Discovery, HGTV, TCM, History, G4 and QVC are just a few examples of networks which provide employment to local actors and voice talent.

And then there is the internet. This baby is just lifting its head off the carpet and starting to crawl. We all know how it's possible to become famous (or infamous) overnight on YouTube. But there are people who are now producing their own shows and making money off of the ad revenue they are generating. That is a whole new ballgame.

In the summer of 2006, 31 year-old Michael Buckley was working as an administrative assistant for a music production company when he decided to host his own comic video program online. Using a video camera, a couple of work lights and a $6 fabric as a backdrop, he started his own celebrity gossip show. Buckley began uploading videos three times a week on YouTube. By September 2008, he was earning a six-figure income through YouTube's partner program, which shares ad revenue with people who upload popular content. Not surprisingly,

Buckley quit his day job. Today, his online show, "What the Buck?" has over a million subscribers.

His story is not unique. Google won't release figures on how much money ad partners earn on average, but in a 2008 New York Times article, a spokesman for the company conceded that "hundreds of YouTube partners are making thousands of dollars a month." How much those figures have risen in the three years since then is any-body's guess. However, there is no question that many people are now making a full-time living off of their own shows on YouTube. And this is just the beginning.

Production houses are now appearing with the sole purpose of creating and distributing videos for the web. Companies such as Maker Studios, Machinima, Mahalo, Vuguru and Next Networks are financed entirely by venture capitalists and grants from Google's You-Tube. All of these studios operate in regional markets, and there are more springing up all the time.

Lisa Donavan is one of the founders of Maker Studios. Better known by her online persona, LisaNova, she initially gained notoriety for her impersonation of Sara Palin – which was uploaded more than a week before Tina Fey performed her own impression on *Saturday Night Live*.

In an interview with the New York Times in April, 2011, Ms. Do-navan was clear about her preference for the web over traditional me-dia: "This feels like this is the future. Trying to get on TV would be going backwards in my mind. It's a waste of time."

It's anybody's guess how fast online productions will continue to encroach upon traditional media, or whether it will eventually replace it altogether, but no one can dispute the fact that they are expanding all the time. That's great news for regional actors, and anyone else inter-ested in making their mark in show business. The internet has created revolutionary opportunities on a level that the entertainment industry has not experienced since the invention of television.

And it's not just the entertainment industry. Today, all corporations consider a strong internet presence a basic necessity. With higher bandwidth, it is now commonplace to see a live actor pop up on-screen when you arrive at a company's home page. Actors welcome the visitor, help them navigate the site, and explain products and services. Typical pay for this sort of thing starts at around $1000 per day for the shoot, plus additional negotiated pay for usage.

Ok, I'm sure you think all this sounds great. Maybe you even think it sounds a little too good to be true. You're probably wondering what the "catch" is. Well, there isn't one, per se. Obviously, I can't guarantee that you will be able to make a living as an actor. It's a competitive business and not everyone can be successful at it. But I can promise you that the odds tilt dramatically in your favor if you live and work in the regional markets.

Of course, it isn't all sunshine and roses. There are downsides to working the regional markets; the biggest being the issue of credibility. The title of this chapter is "The Majority Is Wrong" – and that's exactly how it is. The majority of actors, directors, producers, talent agents, and casting directors believe that if you are a serious actor in the English-speaking world, you live in New York City, Los Angeles or London. Some of these people haven't the vaguest idea that actors even exist outside the major markets – let alone that they are able to make a successful, full-time living at it.

The result of this bias is that you may occasionally lose roles to major market actors who are far less experienced than you are. The reason? Because, contrary to popular belief, the best actor doesn't always get the role; the *most credible* actor does.

Time for another story:

Many years ago I was put on 1st refusal for a national commercial. "1st refusal" simply means they want you to hold the date open. More often than not, you are seriously being considered for a role, but there are still some issues that need to be ironed-out before a final decision is made. In this particular instance, the client and ad agency were trying to decide between me and another actor. Apparently, opinions were divided over which of us should get the role.

It was a great gig. The copy was well-written and the commercial was funny. Furthermore, it was going to be an ongoing campaign. I was living in Atlanta at the time, and it had come down to a choice between me and another young actor/comedian who lived in Los Angeles. In the end, they chose the L.A. actor.

No big deal. You win some, you lose some, right? However, I had made enough of an impression that the ad agency decided to cast me as a supporting character in the commercial (which was, unfortunately, a non-recurring role).

When I arrived on the set, I immediately ran into the actor who had been cast as the lead. I explained who I was, shook his hand and offered my congratulations. Before long, we were chatting away like old friends. After a while, it became obvious that he was nervous and agitated about something, so I asked him about it. Embarrassed, he admitted that it was his first time on the set of *any sort of production*. He was a stand-up comedian – not an actor. He had never performed in front of a camera in his life.

I gave him a crash-course in acting on the spot. Unfortunately, we only had about an hour before we were called to the set. Try as he might, the poor fellow just couldn't relax. As the day wound on, tempers grew short – which only made matters worse. In the end, it was a disaster. The commercial failed to live up to the client's expectations, and the campaign was abandoned altogether.

The lesson? I suppose there are several (particularly for ad agencies), but the one that concerns us most is the issue of credibility. As an actor in the regional markets, you are going to be fighting an uphill battle for credibility with actors in the majors. Even if you work fifty times more than they do (which is entirely possible).

Is it a big deal? No, not really. For the most part, you won't be in competition with them. Even when you are, there is always a chance that common sense will prevail and the ad agency or director will look at your resume, see that you have more experience than 99% of the "wannabe" actors in New York and L.A., realize that you are the more credible option and cast you in the role. It's great when that happens. And it does happen.

It is undeniable that New York and L.A. actors get a certain amount of credibility built-in, just because they live in those cities – even if they rarely work. And while that "credibility edge" is sometimes enough to tip the scales against regional actors, it becomes a moot point when they're up against the competition they face in their own markets.

Therefore, many N.Y. and L.A. actors find themselves locked in a sort of "catch-22". They can't get enough work where they are, but they are afraid to leave the big city and lose what little credibility they have. They see leaving as tantamount to an admission of defeat. They couldn't be more wrong.

What's the point of living "where all the action is", if you can't get a piece of the action? Just because you live in the city where the big game is played doesn't mean you're in the game. It's astonishing how many people in New York and L.A. either don't seem to understand that, or refuse to accept it. Contrary to what most people believe, 95% of "professional" actors in N.Y. and L.A. aren't "in the game" at all. On the contrary; they have taken themselves completely out of the game.

My advice to you? Don't make the same mistake. Stick to the regional markets. Make a consistent living, gain a ton of experience, and quietly cash your checks.

WHAT'S SO GREAT ABOUT REGIONAL MARKETS?

1. *Consistent work* – You improve by doing. In this business, nothing is more credible than performing at a high level, consistently. Whatever credibility you may lose in the short term, you will gain back with interest through experience and hard work.

2. *Repeat business* – Because you will be working in a smaller market, it will be much easier to get repeat business. I have many clients for whom I no longer need to audition. They just call my agent and book me. Nothing could be sweeter.

3. *Gateway to film and TV* – While the masses are fighting it out tooth and nail over day player roles in Los Angeles and New York, those same roles are being cast all over the country. It's infinitely easier to book a day player gig in Michigan (or almost any other state) than it is to book the same role in New York. There's just far less competition.

4. *Lower cost of living* – It goes without saying that if you can keep your costs down, you have a better chance of paying your bills. With less financial pressure, you also tend to relax and perform better.

5. *Less obstacles* – In the regional markets, if you are talented, you will work; it's as simple as that. The same cannot be said for New York or Hollywood.

In the major markets, talent is not enough. Contrary to popular folklore, neither is persistence. I know plenty of Hollywood actors with both. Some have credentials from top acting schools, excellent resumes, and more than their fair share of good looks and charm. A few even have high-level "connections". Despite all of those things, not one of them has been able to make a consistent living as an actor, and some are now into their *third decade* of trying.

Perhaps you think I'm being a bit too negative. After all, who am I to say that it won't happen for them eventually? How do I know they won't get their lucky break tomorrow, or next week?

I'll tell you how I know. Because with each passing day without work, an actor in the major markets becomes less marketable than they were the day before. Remember, this business is all about *credibility*. When you're 19, it is understandable if you don't have much on your resume. It may not be desirable, but at least it's understandable. However, with each passing year, your lack of experience becomes less and less forgivable. Once you go several years without work (and particularly once you are over the age of 25), it is entirely unacceptable. The reasoning here is simple: If you were any good, somebody would have hired you by now. It's tough to argue with that.

This dilemma is further compounded by the fact that the older you get, the tougher your competition becomes. By the time you reach your mid-twenties, you will already be competing with actors who have Broadway credits and leading roles in feature films on their resumes. If all you have done is work at Starbucks – you're in trouble. The problem only gets bigger as you get older. If you still haven't done anything of note by the time you hit your late 20's and early 30's, it's essentially game over. In the major markets, your odds of "making it" do not improve with time – they evaporate.

That is not true of the regional markets. Here, many actors start out in the business late in life and go on to have fantastic careers. That's not to say the smaller markets aren't competitive; they are. But at least it's a manageable level of competition. That makes all the difference in the world.

In 1980, Wilbur Fitzgerald was a 32 year-old trial attorney working for a well-respected firm in Atlanta. Even though the prospects for his career were bright, Wilbur wasn't happy. Law paid the bills, but it wasn't fun or fulfilling, and the thought of devoting the rest of his life to something he didn't enjoy left him feeling empty and depressed.

Wilbur began looking around for something to do in his spare time, and the thought of acting intrigued him. He had no experience with it, other than roleplaying in mock trials as a law student, but he remembered that the roleplaying had been a lot of fun. Almost on a whim, he signed-up for a local acting class.

After years of knuckling down in law school and towing the line in a stuffy legal office, acting struck him like a cool breath of fresh air. Suddenly, he had a reason to cut loose and have fun. It was incredibly liberating – and he was obviously good at it. Within six months of taking his first class, Wilbur booked his first role in an industrial film. From that point on, the work kept coming in. Most of it was for corporations and commercials, but so what? The money was excellent and he was having a ball. He was also gaining a lot of valuable, professional experience.

Wilbur didn't quit his day job right away. He stayed with the law firm for another four years – not because he needed the money, but because he found it hard to let go of something that he had put so much time and effort into. When he finally did make the leap to full-time actor, he instinctively felt as if he had done the right thing.

In 1989, Wilbur auditioned for the role of District Attorney Gerard Darnelle for the television series, "In the Heat of the Night". As you might imagine, the producers were impressed when he mentioned that he had been an attorney in real life. It gave him an edge the other actor's simply couldn't compete with. Wilbur got the part, and went on to appear in 36 episodes over the next six years.

Since then, Wilbur has had recurring roles on shows like Matlock, House of Pain, Friday Night Lights and Prison Break. He's had speaking roles in a wide range of feature films (We are Marshall, The Curious Case of Benjamin Button, Life as We Know It) and has worked with some of the biggest names in Hollywood. Look him up on www.

IMDB.com, and you'll see the kind of career you can have working in the regional markets.

Like me, Wilbur has booked most of his acting jobs while living in Atlanta. Lately, Atlanta has become a hot-spot for acting because of favorable tax-credit laws. These have induced many film and TV shows to move their productions here.

Of course, all of that may have changed by the time you read this. The ongoing battle for Hollywood's business never ends. Another city, state, or country could become the new hot-spot any time. New tax-incentives are constantly being passed by governments all around the country (and world). However, I'm not worried about Hollywood productions leaving for greener pastures, because I was making a great living in Atlanta long before they ever came.

Atlanta is a great place to begin an acting career. However, the same can be said for almost any other major city (other than N.Y and L.A., of course). For that reason, I don't recommend putting yourself through the expense of pulling-up-stakes and chasing after the current hot-spot (wherever it might be); at least not until you've thoroughly explored your options closer to home.

Remember, as the number of acting jobs increases, the level and amount of your competition increases as well. Atlanta is a far more competitive market today than it was just three years ago (before the tax incentives were passed). For that reason, it's harder to make a living as an actor in Atlanta now that it has been at any time in the past.

It's really impossible to say which regional market is "best". There are a myriad of factors to be considered, including your particular type, who your competition is, how good they are, how good you are, the amount of work available, your level of experience, how well you hit-it-off with the agents and casting directors in town, etc…The list goes on and on and on.

There is no "Shangri-La" for actors; where the work is plentiful and the competition non-existent. Wherever you find acting jobs, you will find actors. Each city has its own level of competition and volume of production, and no two places are going to be alike. You may find it impossible make a living in one, but incredibly easy in another. Ideally, you should aim for a location where there is plenty of work for your "type" (whatever that might be), and where you are better than your competition. I can't tell you where that is, but I can all but guarantee you where it is not. The level and amount of competition that you will face in L.A. is so far out of whack with the amount of available work, that it is utterly absurd.

Start close to home. Check out the yellow pages or go online and look for production companies and talent agencies in your area. If you find them, great; if not, broaden the search. There is work *everywhere.* I'm assuming there are businesses where you live? Well, businesses need to advertise, produce training videos and market themselves online. If there are businesses around you, there is a good chance that there is work to be had.

If there are production companies around you, then there is definitely work to be had. Production companies need to produce things in order to stay in business. Just one good relationship with a busy production company could be enough for you to have a full-time acting career.

I once met an actress who lived in a small rural town in southeast Georgia. She told me that there was only one production company anywhere near her. However, she was literally the only actress for miles around. She made a great living as the star in every video they made.

If you live near any major city, there is acting work going on around you right now. And as we move further into an age where business communications, advertising and entertainment demands are increasing daily, it's a safe bet that the demand for quality actors is only going to go up as well. The work is out there. You just have to find it. In a worst-case scenario, you might have to relocate to a larger city in order to get enough work to keep you busy, but that's a small price to pay.

Anywhere is better than Hollywood. I joke with my L.A. friends that they'd have a better chance making it as an actor in Timbuktu. I've never been to Timbuktu, and I don't even know if they have a theatre there, but if not you could always start one. Even if the locals paid you in chickens and eggplants, at least your odds of survival would be fair. That's more than can be said for your chances in Hollywood.

Finding the right market is just the beginning, however. Once you have mapped out your territory, the next thing you will need to work on is your approach to the business.

It's the Opposite

"Acting isn't really a creative profession.
It's an interpretive one."

- Paul Newman

"I tell you this: Something's happening in my life! I did this
"opposite" thing last night. Up was down, black was white,
good was bad, day was night. This has been the dream of my
life – ever since I was a child! And it's all happening because
I am completely ignoring every urge towards common sense
and good judgment I've ever had!"

- George Costanza

My experience in life has been similar to George Costanza's; as soon as I began thinking unconventionally, everything fell into place. For years, acting was the furthest thing from my mind because it seemed like the worst possible choice for someone who wanted to earn a decent living. As it turned out, the opposite was true. It really is a wacky world.

The fact that acting can provide you with a consistent income is merely the first in a long line of opposites when it comes to the realities of this business. For instance, many people are attracted to acting because the idea of being "someone else" appeals to them. Then the first thing they learn in class is that acting is all about *being yourself.* It's a commonly held assumption that in order to be a good actor you need to be a good liar. Nope. Acting is about *being honest.*

Great acting means *not acting.* Instead of *giving it your all,* you should always take care to *hold something back.* This sort of double-speak sounds bizarre and a little Zen-like to the uninitiated. The jargon is further exacerbated by a multitude of acting teachers who seem to go out of their way to foster it (presumably, so that their bemused students will continue to pay them big bucks).

In the last chapter, we saw what a miserable job the average actor is doing of handling their career. In an industry where 95% of the workers are making less than $7000 per year, you obviously don't want to follow along with the herd; not if you plan on eating regularly, anyway. Taking the opposite view of most actors just makes good business sense.

One of the most basic and widely accepted "truths" about acting is that it is hard to do. This impression is reinforced when we hear a top actor referred to as an "artist" or a "genius". On television shows such as *Inside the Actor's Studio,* guest celebrities are given tremendous respect, and all but idolized for their mastery of the craft.

I've never actually met James Lipton, but a close friend of mine has known him for many years and she insists he is a very sweet man. I'm sure she's right. Nevertheless, he drives me nuts. I can't bear to watch him fawn all over his guests. Talented actors or not, they still put their pants on one leg at a time. They're human beings – not demigods.

Idolatry isn't good for anyone. It inflates the actor's ego (the last thing most of them need), and adds an additional layer of intimidation for the students (certainly the last thing they need). It's tough enough to make a living in this business as it is, without building it up to be some kind of unattainable, holier-than-thou art form.

Over the years I have come to notice a rather curious fact. It seems that most actors fall into one of two categories:

1. Those who consider acting to be an art form.
2. Those who consider acting to be a business.

The actors who fall into category number one are definitely the majority. They include the overwhelming number of drama students, part-timers and amateur actors (as well as many former actors who now teach). Those in the second category represent a teeny, tiny minority; the top 2% of actors nationwide.

It's easy to understand why most young actors want to think of themselves as artists. Who doesn't want to be an artist? Everybody knows artists are deep, mysterious and complex. They're cool. People want to date them.

Drama schools and acting teachers understand this too. Perhaps that's why they go out of their way to encourage the belief that acting is a deep, mysterious and complicated art form. Or, maybe it's because most of them have never actually made a living at it themselves and they don't know any better.

I have been fortunate enough to rub shoulders with quite a few working actors in my career; many of whom are far more talented and accomplished than I will ever live to be. I've spoken to scores of them on this subject and I think it's worth noting that, thus far, I have yet to encounter a single one who considers acting to be difficult, mysterious or complicated. Do you think that's a coincidence? I don't.

It seems that while most amateurs, students and teachers hold acting up as an art form; treating it with the reverence and respect one would normally associate with religion; *working* actors take a different view. Indeed, most of the great actors take the exact opposite view. They have what can only be called, a healthy *disrespect* for acting.

You might find that hard to believe, but I can assure you it's the truth. Don't take my word for it though; listen to what some of the biggest names in the history of stage and screen have had to say about it in their own words:

"Acting is the most minor of gifts and not a very high-class way to earn a living. After all, Shirley Temple could do it at the age of four."
- **Katherine Hepburn**

"This is not a tough job. You read a script. If you like the part and the money is O.K., you do it. Then you remember your lines. You show up on time. You do what the director tells you to do."
- **Robert Mitchum**

"Come to work on time, know your lines, and don't bump into the furniture."
- **Spencer Tracy**

"Just let the wardrobe do the acting."
- **Jack Nicholson**

"Method acting? There are quite a few methods. Mine involves a lot of talent, a glass and some cracked ice."
- **John Barrymore**

"Acting is merely the art of keeping a large group of people from coughing."
- **Ralph Richardson**

"Acting is a masochistic form of exhibitionism. It is not quite the occupation of an adult."
- **Laurence Olivier**

"It's a bum's life. Quitting acting; that's a sign of maturity."
- **Marlon Brando**

"Oh yes. I'm an actor, so I just learn my lines, and show up and do it. I gave it a little bit of thought."
- **Anthony Hopkins**

"I don't have technique because I never learnt any."
- Emma Thompson

"I know very little about acting. I'm just an incredibly gifted faker."
- Robert Downey, Jr.

"Acting is farting around in tights."
- Albert Finney

"There's so much crap talked about acting."
- Ben Kingsley

"There's nothing more boring than actors talking about acting."
- James Caan

"In my own mind, I'm not sure that acting is something for a grown man to be doing."
- Steve McQueen

"If you catch me saying 'I am a serious actor,' I beg you to slap me."
- Johnny Depp

"I've always felt that if you can't make money as an actor, you're either incredibly stupid or tragically unlucky."
- John Malkovich

"There's no mystery to it. Nothing more complicated than learning lines and putting on a costume."
- Morgan Freeman

There you have it. The opinions of some of the most celebrated names of stage and screen. They come from a wide range of backgrounds and eras, and yet they all have something in common: They downplay both the importance and difficulty of acting. This is not a minor point.

Professional actors are not entranced by the craft of acting in the same way students, amateurs and teachers seem to be. They are neither in awe of it, nor intimidated by it. Is it possible that their irreverent attitudes have had something to do with their success?

It makes a lot of sense if you think about it. When you downplay the difficulty of something, it becomes easier to handle. Once you accept that something isn't sacred, you are open to challenging the established methods and beliefs surrounding it. A touch of irreverence can be a very healthy thing. It frees you up. It allows you to push boundaries and take greater risks.

Many years ago, I watched Barbara Walters interviewing Marlon Brando for one of her TV specials. I remember it was a major event at the time, because Brando had been a recluse for many years and rarely spoke to the press. During the show, Walters tried to praise him for being one of America's greatest artists, but Brando would have none of it. In fact, he made a point of insisting that acting wasn't an art form at all.

"Then what do you consider art?" Walters asked. "A Rembrandt painting...Mozart chamber music," he replied. What I found most interesting was how much Brando's attitude irritated Walters. It was clear that she was unhappy with his answer. She *wanted* to think of him as an artist.

The self-deprecation that we see in successful actors indicates self-esteem. It takes confidence to laugh at yourself and poke fun at your profession. Confidence is vital in this business. Contrast Brando's approach with that of the typically insecure student or amateur actor, who prattles on about being an "artist" in an effort to impress his friends, or feel better about himself.

Look, if the general public wishes to think of you as an artist, genius or magician performing next-to-impossible tasks, that's fine; so much the better for you. But it is important that you never allow yourself to be swept up in that tide. If you do, your career will almost certainly suffer for it.

Let's say you hit a dry patch and work slows down. Now what?

Well, if you're like most "actor-artists", you're going to start feeling sorry for yourself. Why isn't anyone hiring you? What's wrong with them? Can't they see how talented you are? You'll moan and groan about it to your friends and family, but eventually they'll get tired of hearing it. Nobody wants to be around an insufferable bore for long. So, sooner or later, you'll wind up alone. Maybe then you'll turn to alcohol and drugs for solace. And just like that, another misunderstood, artistic genius will go spiraling down the toilet. If only the world could understand.

Alternatively, you could choose to behave like a professional from day one. That means thinking of yourself as a "product", rather than an "artist". When work slows down for a professional, they don't waste time feeling sorry for themselves. They don't take it personally. A pro gets busy. Professionals know they're running a business, and if their product isn't selling, it's up to them to figure out a way to build demand for it. Instead of moping, pros concentrate their energy into finding ways to make themselves more marketable.

If you want to be an acting student for the rest of your life – by all means, continue with the philosophy that you are a gifted, undiscovered artist. It's your privilege to call yourself whatever you want. But in my opinion, you will be severely undermining your chances of ever making any real money as a professional actor.

Spencer Tracy and the others are right. There is nothing truly difficult about acting. The sooner you strip away the hype and accept that it really isn't much more complicated than showing up on time, knowing your lines and not bumping into the furniture, the sooner you will have a career.

Am I saying that it's so easy anybody can make a living at it? No. That is obviously not the case. Like any professional sport, you need to have the basic skill set to get in the game and then you have to develop those skills in order to compete at a high level. Quality training and practice are important. You're going to have to learn the ropes and that will take time. But you should understand from the beginning that acting isn't rocket science, brain surgery, or quantum physics. Nor is it art. If you want to be an artist, you might want to consider becoming a writer, director or maybe even a cinematographer. Those are all creative professions. This is an interpretive one.

If you want to be a professional actor, do as the great ones do: Develop a healthy *disrespect* for acting. You can still take your work seriously without being overawed or intimidated by it. Don't be afraid to take chances and make mistakes. You are an actor for heaven's sake, not a doctor! Even if you screw up completely, it isn't going to be a disaster. Nobody's going to die. Relax, have fun, and don't be afraid to laugh at yourself.

In my opinion, the reason so many acting students fail to work consistently is that they persist in making a big deal out of what is, essentially, a simple process. The level of competition in professional acting is high; perhaps as high as in most professional sports. If you allow others to convince you that it is also mysterious, complicated and difficult – it will soon become all of those things to you. Once that happens, you're done for.

There is a massive disconnect between the top 2% of actors who are making all the money and the bottom 98% who are struggling to survive – and it isn't simply a matter of income. More often than not, thinking *unlike* the majority of actors just makes good business sense.

In order to illustrate this dichotomy further, I've thrown together a little comparison chart below. This is just an introduction to some of the concepts we will be covering in more detail later, but it should be enough to give you a feel for where we're headed.

Most Actors Say:	But the Top 2% Say:
I am a serious actor.	*I try not to take myself too seriously.*
I am an artist.	*I'm not an artist.*
Acting is really hard.	*Acting is really easy.*
Acting is my life.	*Acting is my job.*
I desperately want that part.	*I can do it, but I don't need it.*
I just need a break.	*I just need an opportunity.*
One day I'll be discovered.	*My career is in my hands.*

To some, this might seem like little more than fancy word-play, but it really goes deeper than that. What we are talking about here is a fundamental difference in philosophy. In many cases, successful actors take the *exact opposite* view of the struggling masses.

What separates the top 2% from the lower 98% isn't really looks, training or talent. It isn't even friends in high places. It is the right mindset.

And that's good news for you. Because it means if you have the basic skills, and are willing to work hard, the biggest impediment standing in the way of your success is going to be your own brain. That is an issue that we can overcome.

NOBODY HIRES A STARVING ACTOR

"Once you've gotten the job, there's nothing to it. If you're an actor, you're an actor. Doing it is not the hard part. The hard part is getting to do it."

- Morgan Freeman

It is the oldest saying in the book. Nearly everyone has heard it at one time or another, but surprisingly few actors take it to heart. If you retain nothing else from these pages, I want you to at least remember this one rule above all others: *Nobody hires a starving actor.*

The concept is simple enough. A starving actor must be a bad actor; otherwise he wouldn't be starving, right? That makes sense. But how can it be of any practical use to us?

In the first instance, we need to recognize that it won't be much good trying to skate by as an actor living paycheck to paycheck. When you're first starting out in this business, unless you have a trust fund, a rich relative or a generous spouse, you're going to need a solid income from some other job source. The traditional choices are waiter and bartender, but personally, I don't recommend either one.

In the first place, waiting and bartending jobs really aren't all that flexible. Schedules tend to come out only a week or two in advance and if you are working, it can be difficult and sometimes impossible to rearrange things at the last minute to make room for an audition, or acting job.

Furthermore, you will almost certainly wind up working a lot of nights, which will not only leave you exhausted during the day, but make it all but impossible for you to do any local theatre in the evenings. This is significant early in your career, because theatre is a great way for you to get noticed and make valuable connections.

Working with a casting director, or helping out at a talent agency is another option. Not only will these jobs serve as crash-courses in how the business works, they are a superb way for you to develop relationships with key people. The main drawbacks are that you will have a somewhat inflexible schedule, the work may only be sporadic, and you will probably be little more than an intern when starting out, so there won't be much money in it for you.

I recommend a job in sales. Something that gives you a local territory and allows you to make appointments and set your own schedule is ideal. Real estate sales, pharmaceutical, medical, office equipment sales or anything like that fits the bill nicely. A sales career holds many advantages for an actor because, at its core, that's what an acting career is really all about – sales.

Oh boy, I can almost hear the protests now: "Sales? I don't want to be a salesman – I hate sales. I didn't decide to become an actor just to be some stupid salesman – I want to be a star…"

Sure you do. But before you can take your turn at bat, you're going to have to prove you can hit, bunt, field and throw. How many times have you seen an actor in a movie or on TV and thought, "That doesn't look so hard. Heck, I could have done that." You might be right.

In fact, there are probably thousands of people who could have done it just as well, or even better. No one will ever know, because none of them were ever in a position to show what they could do. You see, performing the role really isn't the job. Getting hired to play the role in the first place – that's the job.

Therefore, successful acting is, to a large part, dependent upon successful selling. I would even go so far as to say in the early stages of your career, sales training might be more valuable to you than acting lessons, because sales techniques come into play at every stage of the process. From getting an agent, to the audition, to the job (and even long after), you will be selling yourself constantly. A strong sales background will also help you to negotiate effectively. It's called "showbiz" for a reason. The sooner you get yourself into a mindset where you are thinking like a businessperson, the better off you will be.

"How to Master the Art of Selling", by Tom Hopkins is a sales-training classic. It's been around for many years and has recently been updated. Even if you can't find an updated version, the basic techniques that Hopkins discusses in the older versions are timeless and still appropriate. If you have trouble locating a copy, you could also try Zig Zigler. I've never read his work, but I know he has several sales books out there that are highly rated.

To be honest, it doesn't really matter which sales book you read, or what course you take; the basic concepts of successful selling are more or less universal. Just make the effort to learn the fundamentals. I know it doesn't sound like fun, but trust me; it will pay *enormous* dividends throughout your career.

If you already have a second income that you think will be sufficient to support you properly, great. If not, consider that goal to be your number one priority as of this moment. It will be difficult for you to move forward in your acting career in any meaningful way until you accomplish this task. Having a stable form of income is vital; not only because of the inconsistencies of this profession in the early stages of your career, but because it will enable you to present yourself to the industry in the most professional manner possible, right out of the gate.

Which brings me back to where we began: *Nobody hires a starving actor*.

In other words – you can't *need* the role. Ever. If you walk into an audition thinking, "I've got to book this job or I'm not going to be able to pay my light bill", you may as well stop off at a hardware store on the way home to buy a flashlight and some candles. I guarantee you will not book that job. The decision-makers will sense your desperation, and they will avoid you like the plague.

Don't try to kid yourself into believing that you will be able to fake your way through it, either. You won't. It's been estimated that as much as 90% of human communication is non-verbal, and I can certainly believe it. I've been in countless auditions with actors and have seen them expose their needy desperation through their smiles, speech, mannerisms and movements without ever realizing they've done it. It's painful to watch, it's blatantly obvious, and it happens all the time.

Not all starving actors are "starving" because they're short on cash, either. Some just haven't worked in a while and their confidence is low. Some might desperately want a role because it's a really great part, or because they need the credit on their resume. It's all the same. Desperation is desperation. It's a killer every time.

The decision-makers couldn't care less why you need their job. Your needs are not their problem. All they're worried about is how to find the best actor they can lay their hands on. The last thing they want to do is hire a charity case or hard luck story. Therefore, it's to your advantage to make it clear from the beginning that you are neither of those things. One of the most effective ways to do that is by employing "The Takeaway".

The Takeaway simply means that you can increase demand by creating an impression of disinterest, limited supply, or inaccessibility. People want what they can't have. It's a quirky aspect of human nature that women have understood for untold millennia. Young girls employ it whenever they play "hard to get".

The Takeaway isn't merely good for dating, however. Nor is it just an abstract topic for a behavioral economics class. We encounter it in all aspects of our lives on a daily basis. And according to Pauline Wallin, Ph.D.,* there are three very good psychological reasons why it works:

"1. **Heightened Attention**: When something is hard to get (or forbidden) you immediately pay more attention to it. Notice that when you are on a restricted diet, you sometimes get too focused on what you "can't" eat. This heightened attention -- which can escalate into obsession -- makes the forbidden food seem very important...

2. **Perceived Scarcity**: When something is scarce or in short supply, its perceived value increases. You want it more because you think other people also want it...

3. **Psychological Reactance**: People don't like to be told they can't have or can't do something. It's related to not wanting to be controlled by others..."

Women may have been the first to pick up on this rather childish aspect of our human nature, but they certainly aren't the only ones. Ad agencies and salesmen have been using The Takeaway to their advantage for years. How many times have you heard the phrase "For a limited time only", or "Available while supplies last"? These are two examples of it in action, but there are countless others, including:

- A bouncer who prevents people from entering a club in order to create an artificial line outside the front door.

- A girl who makes her ex-boyfriend jealous by ensuring that he sees her with another man.

- A guy who doesn't call a girl for a week after getting her number, even though he's interested in her.

---

* *Taming Your Inner Brat: A Guide for Transforming Self-defeating Behavior* (Wildcat Canyon Press, 2004)

- A salesman who insists he has other buyers eagerly chomping at the bit.

- A politician who keeps a foreign dignitary waiting for him on purpose.

- A businessman who says that he has to check his appointment calendar, even though he knows it's empty.

- A restaurant charging exorbitant prices in order to appear "exclusive".

The Takeaway is everywhere, and it's especially prevalent in the upper echelons of this business. All Hollywood managers and agents live by it. The top 2% actors use it all the time (even though they may not have a name for it), and you need to use it too.

There's no magic to The Takeaway. Once you're aware of it, it becomes second nature. We'll cover it much more extensively when we get into the chapter on "Perception". I only bring it up now to introduce you to the concept and further illustrate the sharp contrast between the attitudes of the top 2% and the struggling majority.

Imagine the typical actor walking into an audition. Naturally, he wants to do well. Perhaps he needs the money, or maybe it's just a good role and he doesn't want to blow it. Either way, he's putting pressure on himself, so he's extra nervous. He's desperate to make a great impression and eager to show everyone that he's funny, friendly, energetic and enthusiastic. Unfortunately, he only has about 60 seconds in which to do all of those things. Meanwhile, he still has an audition to perform…

When you try to be all things to all people in just under a minute, it's tough to avoid looking desperate, insecure and maybe even a little ridiculous. These are not traits that inspire confidence. Nor are they normally associated with professionalism.

Imagine a businessman on the street who is approached by a beggar, or a traveling salesman showing up at the front door of someone's home, or even a pretty girl confronted with a secret admirer. In each of these situations, one person holds all the cards, and the other is desperate and needy. Interestingly, the person with all the power is often the one who is the most uncomfortable. Usually, they just want the encounter to be over with as quickly as possible.

Is that how you want the people observing you in an audition to feel? Then don't give them a reason to! Play a little Takeaway instead. Walk in, say "hi", hit your mark and do your thing. When the audition is over, smile, say "thanks" and walk out. If they want to strike up a conversation with you, engage them. Otherwise, stay focused on the task at hand. Your performance will be better for it. Meanwhile, your manner and body language will be saying, "Look, I'm a pro. I'm happy to do this for you, but if you don't think I'm right for the part – so be it. I really don't need this gig anyway. I have more than enough things going on to keep me busy as it is."

A lot of actors are afraid to do this because they're concerned that they might come across as cold or unsociable. I'm not advising you to be surly, arrogant, or walk in looking like you just left a funeral. You can smile and be pleasant to people without gushing all over them, or kissing their asses.

Treat them as your peers, because that's really what they are. The same goes for agents, managers, and anybody else you meet in this business – including major movie stars. The relationship should always be "professional meets professional", and never "beggar meets king".

Nobody hires a starving actor. Never forget it.

FIRST STEPS

Before you embark upon an acting career, there are a few things you're going to need in your arsenal: Great headshots, a resume and monologues.

I'm not going to spend too much time covering the basics with regards to these since there's a boat-load of information on the internet readily available via a quick search. Instead, I'd like to touch on each of them briefly, just to give you a few pointers.

First, you will need professional headshots. Make sure you have them taken by a *professional headshot photographer*. Other than training, headshots are the single biggest expense for an actor, so it's understandable that this is where many try to save a few bucks by enlisting the help of friends or amateur photographers. Bad move.

Again, in keeping with our ongoing theme, we don't want to do what most actors do. Don't think of your headshots as mere photos. Headshots are a billboard for your entire business; they are a two-dimensional indication to the world of just how professional (or unprofessional) you are.

Headshots project your image; and in this business, image really is everything. For that reason, you want the best damned headshots money can buy. If you think you can't afford to buy top-of-the-line headshots, you're wrong. You can't afford not to. Great headshots will pay for themselves many, many times over.

Think about it this way: Great headshots are like having a team of assistants hustling for you around the clock, 24 hours a day. No matter where you are or what you happen to be doing; your little assistants are out there circulating in the world, trying their best to make you look good.

Cheap headshots are like hiring lazy bums to work for you. What's the point? They won't do the job you've hired them for and they're going to make a bad impression on everyone who sees them. They may even *cost* you jobs. And when your back is turned, your crappy headshots are out there telling everybody what a cheap, starving actor you are. Can you afford that?

Research photographers online and compare their work. Although more expensive doesn't always mean better, it usually does. If you can't find an excellent headshot photographer in your area, bite the bullet and fly to New York or Los Angeles to have them done. Most top photographers in the major markets will charge between $400 and $600 for a session. You can take a mini-vacation at the same time and write the whole thing off on your taxes. One decent job pays for it all; and with your brand-new, top-notch photos, your chances of landing that job will increase. You don't have to be a major-market actor, but that doesn't mean you shouldn't look like one.

Believe me, I'm not the sort of person who enjoys tossing money away for no good reason. But as the old saying goes, sometimes it takes money to make money. If you're serious about acting as a career, then you need to be serious about approaching it as a business, too. There aren't many legitimate businesses where your startup costs will be less than they are here. It's worth the investment.

Another reason for you to get great headshots at the beginning of your career is to off-set the rather limited resume you're going to be starting out with. In the beginning, your resume will be your Achilles heel. You will want those dynamite photos to pick up the slack.

After you get the shots back from the session, be sure to get lots of opinions before you decide which one(s) to print. It's hard to judge your own photos objectively, and we often think we look good when we don't. Be sure to get opinions from people of the opposite sex, as well as your friends, family and agent, if applicable.

The most important thing to keep in mind is that the shots must look like you. If you show them to people and they say, "Wow, you look amazing here; I would have never recognized you..." That's not good. It's pointless looking ten years younger in your headshot if you're going to walk into an audition and look ten years older in person.

Once you decide on a photo (or photos), the next thing you're going to have to do is print copies. There are lots of places that will do this for you online and there are probably a few local shops near you that will do it as well. Just be sure to pick a company that's used to printing headshots.

There is often some debate among actors over whether they should order prints or lithograph copies. As far as I'm concerned, there is no contest. Get lithographs. Prints are expensive, they tend to curl up, and it's difficult (if not impossible) to print your resume on the back of them.

The counter-argument in favor of prints is that directors are usually photographers (true) and that it makes a huge difference to them (false). Directors couldn't care less. They're concerned with the image, not what it's printed on.

Another bone of contention: I've noticed actors online asking whether it's alright to staple their resumes to the back of their headshots, and a lot of the crusty old vets are saying that it's perfectly fine. Well, *it is* fine in the sense that no one is going to toss your photo in the trash just because your resume is stapled to it, but it *is not* fine in the respect that it instantly flags you as a cheap, starving actor who has nothing better to do than sit at home for hours-on-end cutting and stapling resumes. Folks, you can pick up a quality printer for about $80 these days. There are no excuses.

Speaking of resumes, there are standardized layouts which you will want to adhere to. Again, a lot of info is available on the web.

Basically, you want to list film credits first, followed by television, commercial, theatrical and industrial credits. Then list any training and special skills. New Yorkers prefer to list theatrical credits first. When in doubt, I advise you to lead off with your best (and hopefully most recent) stuff up top.

The question I am most often asked with regards to resumes is whether it is acceptable to "pad" it with false credits. My personal belief is that honesty is the best policy.

When I first started out, the only thing I had on my resume was the fact that I played a duck in elementary school. The rest of the page was completely blank. I had a high-quality headshot, but the flip-side was like a bad joke.

As a matter of fact, it did get some laughs and worked out pretty well for me. It was a conversation starter. It also served as a little bit of a Takeaway in auditions, since it showed I had a sense of humor and didn't give a damn what anybody thought. I wound up keeping it on there for a number of years – even after my resume started to fill up with legitimate work.

Although you may feel a little insecure about your lack of credits, it won't seem like such a big deal to a good director, especially if you're young and/or right for the part. Everyone has to start out somewhere, and people get a thrill out of coming across a hot new talent. Give yourself some time. Better that than the humiliation and loss of credibility that you will suffer if you get caught in a lie. That's my opinion anyway. Take it or ignore it as you wish. Just be prepared to face the music if you get busted.

Last but not least, you're going to need to learn a least two contemporary monologues; one comedic and one dramatic. There are a great many books that specialize in monologues for men and women. Pick up a few of those and choose something you like. You could always learn a classical monologue as well, of course – but you will probably only use it when auditioning for a classical play. Unless you're reading for a lot of Shakespearian productions, your contemporary monologues will be your bread and butter.

If you have a favorite monologue from a popular movie, I would not advise using it for auditions. Chances are good that you're going to wind up looking like a bad actor – even if you can perform it better than the person in the film. That's because they will have had the benefit of an entire production behind them – director, cinematographer, lighting, music, makeup, editing…and all you will have is yourself. It's a stacked deck and it isn't going to work in your favor.

Also, stay away from "story" monologues where you sit and talk about something that happened in the past. These tend to be difficult for beginners. A much better choice is an active monologue between you and someone else. Treat it as a dialogue, just don't let the other "person" get a word in.

When delivering your monologue in an audition situation, avoid making eye contact with the people for whom you're auditioning. Doing so is called "breaking the fourth wall". There are instances where this can be desirable (such as in a soliloquy), but in an audition it isn't a good thing, because you ruin the auditors' immersion by pulling them into your scene. Engaging your audience directly makes it hard for them to observe you objectively.

Instead, pick a small spot on the wall behind them, and use that as the person with whom you are conversing. Don't just talk to the spot; use your imagination to really "see" the person. If you have trouble seeing someone clearly, then you're going to have to give your imagination some help.

To do this, find a photograph ahead of time and use that as the basis of your conversation. It doesn't matter whose photograph you use – it could be a family member, a friend or just some random photo off the internet. Study the image closely. Note the color of the eyes, hair, clothes and posture – as well as the mood of the individual. When you are performing your monologue, this is the person you will be talking to. Imagine them standing in front of you exactly as they were in the photograph. In this way, your eyes will register an actual picture. That is more convincing than trying to conjure a vague image out of thin air.

As you progress through the scene, imagine the other person reacting to what you are saying. Perhaps at some point they will try to speak – and you won't let them. Keep your focus on *them*. If you find you are overly conscious of your hands, facial expressions or body in any way, then you aren't communicating your message effectively enough. Keep the focus on who you're talking to and what you're fighting for. See them, listen to them, and react.

The last bit of advice I want to give you in these initial stages of launching your career is to take the time to seek out a mentor. This is easier than you might think. All you need to do is start asking questions. How do I get into acting? Where do I start? Who are the best actors in town? And so on. Questions have a way of leading to more questions – which eventually lead to people who have the answers.

Everyone loves enthusiasm. If you're passionate and eager to become an actor, you will make a lot of friends and you will get a ton of free advice. Remember, much of this is going to be *bad* advice. Let this book be your guide as you attempt to sift the wheat from the chaff.

If someone wants to take you under their wing and teach you the ropes, as long as they're accomplished and successful, let them! However, don't try to push people into such a position, and take care not to make a nuisance of yourself. After all, actors have their own careers, families and lives to think about.

If you have talent, it will not be long before it is recognized. You'll be amazed by the number of people who will be willing to help out in any way they can – even though you might end up being a direct competitor of theirs. Believe it or not, the majority of people in this industry are kind-hearted, complimentary, and supportive of talent when they see it.

Training

"There are children playing in the streets who could solve some of my top problems in physics, because they have modes of sensory perception that I lost long ago."
- J. Robert Oppenheimer

"The best actors, I think, have a childlike quality. They have a sort of an ability to lose themselves."
- Kenneth Branagh

"I enjoyed being in movies when I was a boy. As a child you're not acting – you believe."
- Roddy McDowall

A strange thing happens to people when you point a camera at them: They change. Some throw back their shoulders and suck in their bellies; others fidget, adjust their clothes or stiffen-up. Many try to mold their facial expression and/or physique in a way that shows them off to best advantage. Still others prefer to shy away from the camera altogether, turning their heads or flinging up a hand to prevent their image from being captured. By contrast, when you point a camera at a young child, something completely different happens: Nothing.

Kids don't change at all. You have to direct them every step of the way. Children have to be told to stand up straight, put down their toys, take their hands out of their pockets, stop picking their noses, look up at mommy and smile. If you don't tell them to do these things, they will just carry on being themselves.

The same is true of a dog. Oh, he might look up at you quizzically, wondering why you are pointing that strange object at him and speaking in such a high, friendly tone of voice – but he'll never be vain. I've yet to see a dog suck in his belly or worry about how he looked on camera. And when you show them a photo of themselves afterwards, most dogs couldn't care less.

Kids and animals aren't self-conscious in front of a camera because they have no trace of self-consciousness in their normal, everyday lives. This is why they make such compelling performers.

The great promoter, W.C. Fields once advised, "Never work with children or animals", and it's still a good rule of thumb. Not because children and animals are particularly difficult to work with (they aren't), but because they are so much better at it than we adults are. After filming "The Sixth Sense", Bruce Willis said he learned more about acting from his ten-year old co-star (Haley Joel Osment) than in any class he ever took in his life. I can believe it.

When my nieces and nephews were young, we used to play a game where I was the "monster" trying to catch them. I never had to instruct the kids on how to "act" frightened. Fear is one of the most difficult emotions for an adult actor to portray, but children seem to be able to pull it off without any training at all. Watching them scrambling around; arms flailing in the air, screaming like a pack of wild banshees – you could be forgiven for thinking they were being chased by a real werewolf instead of their favorite uncle. They were convincing, not because they were *acting* afraid, but because they *really were afraid.* I know that to be true, because whenever I managed to catch one, I could feel their heartbeats racing with panic.

Think about that: Their imaginations were so vivid that they actually fooled their own nervous systems! As a result, their bodies physically reacted as if the danger was real – even to the point where their adrenaline surged and their pulses raced. As far as their minds and bodies were concerned, they were in real peril. I didn't have to put on scary makeup or a costume in order to get that reaction out of them, either. An active imagination can be an incredibly powerful thing.

The challenge for us as adult actors is to re-awaken our forgotten, childhood imaginations. That might be easier for some than others, but everyone should be capable of doing it. After all, we were all children once. We all experienced what it felt like to have a monster hiding in our closet or lurking under our bed. Surely, everyone spent at least one night under the covers, paralyzed with fear; hearts pounding, palms sweaty, startled by the slightest sound. It was all in our minds of course, but it certainly seemed real at the time. That was a powerful imagination at work. If we had it once, we can have it again.

Similarly, we must fight to overcome our self-consciousness and get back to the way we used to be, when we were more interested in what was going on around us, than ourselves. Don't think of acting as a set of rules or laws that you need to study, memorize and master. That isn't it at all. Learning how to act is more about *unlearning* all the bad habits that you have been accumulating since puberty.

Reading, speaking and imagination are the core skills that you should always be developing. Think of these as your foundation. All the rest is a matter of discarding unwanted baggage in order to set the actor within you free. Good training will help you do that.

Fully training you as an actor is beyond the scope of this book, or any other book for that matter. Reading about it can only take you so far. At some point, you have to jump in and get your feet wet. That can be accomplished in several different ways.

Drama School

Many people are interested in acting at an early age. Naturally, one of their first steps is to join a drama classes in high school or college. Unfortunately, the overwhelming majority of instructors at these institutions have little or no professional acting experience. The result is that many bad habits are taught in drama classes around the country. Some of these are not so easy to break. We will cover those issues in detail later. For now, it is enough for you to know that it is possible to have a successful acting career without studying drama in high school or college. However, if you have your heart set on pursuing a degree, I recommend attending a nationally recognized school, where you can at least be sure you are going to be well trained.

The top three drama programs in the United States are considered to be the undergraduate degree at Juilliard, and the MFA programs offered by Yale and NYU. While none of these programs comes with any kind of guarantee that you will be able to work professionally, there is no question that each carries a lot of credibility within the industry. When agents see these programs on a resume, they sit up and take notice. If I had to choose one of them for my own child, I would pick the Juilliard program as the most desirable. Not because it's better training per se, but because the degree can be obtained at a younger age.

Of course, there are other highly regarded drama programs throughout the U.S., such as those offered by Carnegie Mellon, USC and UNC School of the Arts, among others. Each spring, graduates from top drama schools all across the country take part in showcases in New York City called, "The Leagues". The Leagues are widely attended by top agents and casting directors, but the greatest attention and interest still seems to be reserved for the "big three" of Yale, Julliard and NYU.

If the thought of studying in London appeals to you, you could always shoot for LAMBDA (the London Academy of Dramatic Arts) or

RADA (the Royal Academy of Dramatic Arts). Both have reputations for producing some of the finest actors in the world. If I could start my life all over again, I would take a shot at getting into LAMBDA or RADA. However, I should qualify that by saying I hold dual-nationality and I am an English citizen. That's a significant factor. If you have the ability to live and work in England – go for it. Otherwise, you might be better off obtaining a degree in your own country, where you will have a better chance of making connections that could benefit your career later on.

For U.S. citizens, I would recommend sticking to the league schools; preferably one that requires you to pass an audition in order to be accepted. Schools that don't weed-out applicants will accept anyone willing to pay the cost of their tuition. That might sound appealing to a youngster intimidated by the audition process, but it's a fear that must be overcome sooner or later. I'd be wary of investing my time and money in a program that had no means of filtering out substandard candidates.

Besides the financial cost of a degree, there is also an opportunity cost which must be considered. During the years you will be studying, you will effectively be taking yourself "off the market". In other words, you will be missing out on acting jobs that you could have auditioned for had you not been in school. Is that tradeoff worth it? No one can say for sure, since it is anybody's guess what opportunities (if any) you will miss.

Speaking for myself, I can honestly say that in two decades as a working professional, I don't know of a single instance where not having a drama degree has cost me a job. Maybe it has somewhere along the line – but I doubt it. The issue has certainly never come up in an audition or interview situation. Is it possible that, had I completed a top program at a young age, I might be a more accomplished actor today? Of course. Anything's possible. All I can say is that I'm satisfied with the way my career has turned out so far, and that I have no real regrets.

Drama school isn't for everyone. Then again, neither is professional acting. There are many who will want to study drama simply for the love of it and there's certainly nothing wrong with that. I'm a big fan of people who pursue their passion.

With a drama degree, even if you never "make it" as an actor, you could always wind up doing something else related to the industry, such as costume, makeup, set-design, lighting, production, stage management, special effects and so on. You could also write, teach or direct. Who knows? You might even open a theatre of your own one day.

Money isn't everything, and acting for the camera isn't the only career worth pursuing. However, it happens to be the focus of this book, so forgive me if I jump to the conclusion that it's the real reason you're here. Before committing thousands of dollars and years of your life to a drama degree, you should understand that you need to be choosy about where you go, and realize that even the best institutions don't come with any kind of a guarantee.

SCENE STUDY CLASSES

It is possible to obtain excellent training outside of a college curriculum. Ongoing classes abound in every major city in the U.S., and a great many minor ones, too. These classes usually focus on auditions, scene study or both. The most important factor in choosing a class is the instructor. Who are they and what have they done? Can you trust their opinion?

You will rarely encounter an acting teacher who thinks like a top 2% actor. The best ones do, but most do not. This is understandable, since many teach acting who cannot make a living at it themselves. However, the fact that someone was never a top actor isn't a good enough reason to write them off as a teacher. They may still have valuable lessons for you. There are many fine teachers who cannot make a living as actors, just as there are a lot of fine actors that would make perfectly lousy teachers. The important thing to remember is that nobody's word is sacred. Never be afraid to question your teacher, or their methods.

Great teachers don't mind being challenged. In fact, they welcome the feedback and open discussion. It lets them know that their students are paying attention and that they're processing the information. The best instructors communicate well and find ways to challenge their students, without demoralizing them. Their underlying goal is to build *confidence.*

Bad teachers come in many forms. Some behave as if they are the gatekeepers to the secret world of acting. They deliver their message in abstract terminology. They complicate the simple in an effort to make themselves look wise. Their underlying goal is to build *dependency.*

Such classes exist to serve the financial and emotional needs of the instructor, rather than the students. I don't know about you, but if I'm going to pay someone to teach me how to do something, I expect the matter to be clarified by their instruction – not obscured by it. If I wind-up more confused than when I began, there is a problem somewhere. Either I am a bad student, or they are a bad teacher. Either way, I'm wasting my time and money.

Be cautious of teachers who try to hook you into becoming a perennial student. It's obviously great for them if you attend their classes once a week for the next five years of your life, but is it good for you? You want an instructor, not a Svengali.

A good acting class will build your confidence. It will make you feel energized and empowered. A bad one will leave you confused and demoralized. If you find that your confidence and self-esteem are taking a beating, leave the class. It's hurting more than it's helping.

Finding a good class is a little bit like falling in love. When it happens, you will know. However, no matter how knowledgeable and wise the teacher is, it stands to reason that sooner or later you're going to master their methods. Once that happens, they are going to run out of things to teach you. When you feel as though you are no longer improving, or that you have become "the star of the class", it is time for you to move on.

Many actors resist this. Instead, they continue to study in an ongoing acting class long after they've learned everything the instructor has to offer them. Often, this is because they have become close friends with their teacher or classmates, and they feel attached. I'm not advising you to abandon your friends – just the class.

Some continue attending classes because they see them as a kind of "therapy". This is a huge and potentially dangerous mistake. Acting isn't therapy. Nor is it a viable substitute for therapy. If you think you need therapy, go and see a therapist.

Ongoing acting classes are like a bell-curve; in the early stages, you make huge gains as your mind opens up to new concepts. As you master them, your progress begins to slow down and level off. Eventually, it ceases altogether. When you have reached the top of the curve, it is time for you to leave the class. From that point on, the journey is all downhill. It's a strange phenomenon, but I've seen it happen time and time again. I have known many actors (myself included) who have remained in an ongoing class longer than they should. The result is that progression turns to regression, confidence begins to waver, and confusion starts to creep in. Even the best instructor can only teach you so much. Once you have mastered their methods, all that is left for them to do is nitpick and find fault – often where there isn't any to be found. That is demoralizing for a student.

What teachers *should* do is concede that their students have mastered their techniques and allow them to "graduate" from the class. In reality, few do this because they want the student's money. Therefore, it is up to the student to "graduate themselves" before the downhill journey begins.

Perhaps the reason most often cited by actors for continuing to attend classes, even after they have learned all there is to learn, is that they feel the classes help them to stay "sharp" and "in-tune"; much like regular workouts at a gym. That's fair enough, but there is still a risk of acting in a bubble. In other words, the work looks great in the classroom because everyone is using the same set of rules. But out in the real world, it's a different story. The work appears "forced" or "mechanical".

If you wish to keep studying in order to stay sharp, at least change up the classes and instructors now and then. It's important to maintain a fresh perspective and get new opinions. The questions you should always be asking yourself as a student are:

1. Am I learning anything of value?

2. Are things becoming clearer, or more confusing?

3. Am I gaining confidence, or losing it?

If the class is working for you, great. Stick with it for a while – but don't plan on being there forever. Everyone has to leave the nest eventually, no matter how safe and cozy it might be. Your confidence as an actor can never fully develop until you muster the courage to spread your wings and strike out on your own. You will have victories, and you will have failures, but they must be *your* victories and failures – not your instructor's.

WORKSHOPS

Today, many acting classes are taught in the form of weekend workshops. With the right instructor, these can be good value and well worth the investment in time and money. With the wrong instructor, they are a waste of both.

Many workshops are taught by casting directors. That isn't necessarily a bad thing; casting directors have seen a lot of actors perform and they have a good sense of what works in an audition and what doesn't. Just keep in mind that casting directors are neither directors nor actors. In fact, they are often untrained in either discipline.

In spite of their title, casting directors rarely cast anybody in anything. It is usually a director, producer, ad agent or client who decides which actor gets cast – not the casting director. The job of a casting director is to assemble the talent, not develop it.

Paying a casting director to teach you how to act is a little bit like hiring a real estate appraiser to design and build your home. An appraiser might be able to tell you how much a house is worth, but what do they know about architecture and construction?

Most actors understand that perfectly well. For the most part, they pay to take a casting director's workshop simply as a way to meet the individual and show off what they can do. If this is your plan, I recommend that you wait until you are completely confident of your abilities. First impressions are often lasting ones. If you take a workshop with a casting director and come across looking like a rank amateur, it could be a long time before they ever give you another chance.

In my opinion, the best way to meet a casting director is not by taking one of their workshops, but by having your agent submit you to one of their auditions. That way, they see you as a pro right from the beginning. Casting directors are no different than anyone else in this business; when given a choice, they will pick professionals over amateurs every time. For that reason, it is often in your best interest to make sure that you are an established pro before you step in front of them.

IMPROVISATIONAL TRAINING

"If you want to improve, be content to be thought foolish and stupid."
- Epictetus (Greek Stoic Philosopher)

I recently had a conversation with a commercial casting director who told me about an interesting development that has been taking place over the last couple of years. It seems more and more ad agencies are requesting "real people" for their commercials instead of actors. The reason? Apparently, they can't get the actors to stop acting. Seriously, I am not making that up.

The popularity of reality TV, *YouTube* and improvised productions such as *"The Office"*, *"Curb Your Enthusiasm"* and *"Borat"* have set new standards for what "real" means to an audience today. The acting in old television shows and commercials now looks stiff, stilted and contrived by comparison. Audiences are clamoring for more *reality* in their acting, and they aren't the only ones; directors, producers and ad agencies are demanding it as well. Like it or not – improv is here to stay.

Does this mean actors aren't going to be able to find work anymore? No, of course not. It just means the actors who do not seem real are not going to find work. Actors will always be in demand, because the problem with putting a non-actor in front of a camera is that you all-too-often end up with the sort of nightmare situation I referred to earlier, where a person just panics and freezes up. What these ad agencies and directors really want (whether or not they realize it) are actors who can act so naturally and realistically, that you cannot tell they're acting.

This is why improvisational actors are in such high demand. Even when a show is not specifically designed to be improvised, directors, ad agents and producers still love to hire actors who have improv ability because they like knowing the option to improvise is available to them. When I shot "Meet the Browns", Tyler Perry decided to throw our script out at the last minute, and we had to improvise our scene entirely. That sort of thing is becoming more and more common, and you have to be prepared for it. One of the best ways you can do that is by taking a comedy improv class.

If you're thinking, "I want to be an actor, not a comedian..." I hear you, and I sympathize. At one time I felt exactly the same way. However, over the years, I have worked with a great many actors with comedy improv experience, and I am consistently struck by the fact that I can immediately tell the difference.

I think it is because people who have a background in comedy improv are so used to performing without a script and relying on their wits alone, that they develop an aura of fearlessness. They know they can handle anything that comes up, because they have done it so many times before. This gives them an enormous boost in confidence. Their acting seems alert, alive and "in the moment". They listen well and re-act naturally. These are the things improvisation teaches you. They are the qualities that every actor should have, but so few actually possess.

So don't think of this as a test of *funny* – think of it as a test of *courage*. Actually, the most frightening part about comedy improv is signing up for the class in the first place. After that, it really isn't scary at all; it's a lot of fun. It teaches you to relax on stage and trust yourself. There are no lines for you to forget and therefore no way for you to screw up. Much like dancing the tango – if you get tangled up, you just tango on.

In a classroom setting, there won't be any pressure on you to be funny, so don't worry about it. Nobody cares. Being funny isn't the object at all. This is about becoming an actor, not a comedian. It's about pushing yourself and finding out what you're capable of. Improv training is all about teaching you how to listen, live in the moment, and react honestly. It will also teach you how to bring more drama into a scene. It really is vital training for any actor – now more than ever.

Actors with improv experience are in major demand. Trust me, if you only have one form of training on your resume, it needs to be comedy improv. It's some of the most useful and valuable training you will find at any price. Give it a try. And don't worry about making a fool out of yourself. Even if you fall flat on your face, at least you are still moving forward.

EMOTIONAL RECALL CLASSES

Throughout most of human history, having a bunch of eyeballs staring at you has not been a good thing. For the most part, it meant you were about to be attacked and possibly even eaten. Perhaps that is why we humans are so sensitive about being watched. Try staring as someone in a shopping mall or on the subway and see how long it takes them to notice what you're doing (and get pissed off). Most people can spot an individual staring at them in a matter of seconds – even in a crowded room.

Being watched makes us uncomfortable. Public speaking is the number one fear among adults. When most people stand up in front of an audience, they become acutely aware of being "looked at". They get stiff, nervous, and start to do things like swing their arms, tap their feet or repeatedly clear their throat.

Self-conscious movements like these originate in the somatic nervous system and are called, *voluntary responses*. What that means is that our minds have to send specific instructions to certain muscles groups in order for these motions to occur. Even though a person may be unaware of them, the movements are all "voluntary". With a little bit of practice, they can be controlled.

On the other hand, our bodies are also subject to *involuntary responses*. These responses are activated by the autonomic nervous system and they don't require any conscious thought in order to occur. A heartbeat would be an example of an involuntary response. Sleeping, sweating and our emotions are others.

Involuntary responses are uncontrollable; however, they can sometimes be induced or stimulated. An audience intuitively understands this (if not the science behind it), which is why actors who show genuine emotions in a performance are so highly praised. Showing real emotions is probably the hardest thing an actor ever has to do. It is impressive, and I think it is the main reason so many people are intimidated by this business. I have occasionally had people tell me that they would like to try acting, but are afraid they wouldn't be any good at it because they can't cry on cue.

If this is something you are concerned about, let me put your mind as ease. There are several reasons why you don't need to worry about generating real emotions in the beginning of your career. The first is that you will rarely be asked to do it.

In commercials, you need to be pleasant, sincere and perhaps enthusiastic. There are very few tears in commercials. Occasionally, you might have to be frustrated or annoyed, but since most of us experience those feelings on a semi-regular basis, that shouldn't pose too much of a challenge for you.

Even in film and television, the overwhelming majority of roles call for little or no genuine emotions. In an entire feature, the lead might have one or two scenes at best, while the supporting characters will often have none at all. Pick any TV show or movie you like: Ninety percent of it is going to be actors walking and talking and trying not to bump into the furniture.

But what if lightning strikes? Suppose your agent calls you up and asks you to read for a role that *does* call for emotions which you are incapable of inducing? Surely it will happen to you eventually?

Maybe. It has happened to me a few times. Just do your best. Try to immerse yourself in the role as best you can. Don't attempt to force the emotions out. Let whatever happens, happen.

I never try to make myself cry. People don't do that in real life anyway; they try *not* to do it. If I have to audition for a scene where I'm supposed to cry, I go in telling myself that I'm not going to let it happen. Sometimes I succeed, sometimes I fail. Either way, it isn't important. What matters most is that I'm listening, and being honest.

If a role calls for emotions that you are incapable of producing, you're not going to get the part, so it's really a moot point anyway. Nobody is ever going to cast you in a part that calls for emotions you are incapable of showing, so why make yourself sick about it? There are plenty of other roles out there that are more suited to your abilities. Better to focus your energies on the things you can do.

Of course, we would all like to be able to do everything brilliantly, but that simply isn't impossible. Everyone has their own strengths and limitations. There is no shame in acknowledging that. Lots of actors can cry on cue. If you are one of them, terrific; it is a feather in your cap. If not, don't worry about it. It isn't that big of a deal.

Don't be afraid to turn down a role if you feel it's something you can't do, or don't want to do. This is your livelihood and it's up to you to decide the boundaries. Some actors have no problem getting naked in front of the camera, while others refuse. It's up to you. Turning down work isn't a sin. On the contrary; as we shall soon see, it can sometimes be good for business.

Why should you base all of your early training around the most difficult thing an actor ever has to do, which will rarely be useful in the early stages of your career anyway? It doesn't make any logical sense. When you are learning something new, there has to be an order to the process. You have to learn how to walk before you can run. Jumping into an emotional recall class when you are first starting out as an actor is like trying to surf before you can stand. It's a safe bet that you're going to wipeout.

It is pointless trying to master *involuntary* responses when you have not yet learned how to control the *voluntary* ones. Your first goal as an actor is to learn how to stand, sit, talk, and at all times "be your-self" with the public eye (or camera) upon you. That takes time. Don't worry about expanding your repertoire until you have mastered this first stage.

Stay away from emotional recall classes, at least for now. You won't need them starting out, and there is a good chance that if you jump in too soon, you will begin focusing on all the wrong things. That's how young actors get confused and discouraged. Instead, keep it simple and stick to what you are good at; being you.

OTHER STUFF

Anything you can do to build self-confidence is great for your career. Confidence comes from overcoming obstacles, so you must be willing to challenge yourself. We've already talked about how basic acting and improv classes are great for that, but there are many other things you can do outside of acting. Consider taking up a sport. Activities such as tennis, soccer, golf, mountain biking, rock climbing, martial arts, yoga, ballroom dancing, horseback riding and fencing can pay dividends for you many times over. Apart from raising self-esteem, they will also improve your health and physical appearance. As a general rule; healthy actors tend to work more often.

Any activity that you're particularly good at should be listed as a skill on your resume. Many an actor has landed a role simply because they could surf, rollerblade or ride a motorcycle. Skills make you more marketable and interesting. The more interesting and marketable you are, the more in-demand you will be.

Finally, you need to keep working on those core skills: Reading, speaking and imagination. As far as I'm concerned, you should consider reading as much a part of your training regime as acting classes, sales courses or going to the gym. In fact, it will probably have a greater impact on your career than any of those things.

CRASH COURSE: ACTING 101

"Mediocrity knows nothing higher than itself, but talent instantly recognizes genius."

- Arthur Conan Doyle

"I don't honestly think people know what acting is."

- Ben Kingsley

If you aspire to be a great actor, you will need to learn to recognize great acting when you see it. It is reasonable to assume that a person who has watched thousands of movies *should* be able to spot great acting when it pops up in front of them, but in my experience, that is not always the case. In fact, it is almost impossible for the average moviegoer to isolate an actor's performance and judge it on its own merits. There are too many other factors coming into play: Direction, music, editing, camera work, script, the actor's physical appearance, lighting, etc...

The greatest actor in the world can be made to look a fool with bad writing, directing or editing. On the other hand, top-notch writing, directing and editing can make a mediocre actor look like a genius. The truth is that actors are just one small piece of the production puzzle. For the most part, we get too much credit when a film succeeds and too much blame when it flops.

Not long ago, I was discussing the subject of acting with a favorite uncle of mine. He's a major movie buff and a huge fan of Robert De Niro. He brought up the massive physical transformation that De Niro went through in "Raging Bull" as evidence of what a great actor he is. Many other actors have undertaken similarly impressive transformations: Demi Moore in "GI Jane"; Christian Bale in "The Fighter"; and Mickey Rourke in "The Wrestler" are three who leap to mind. There are others of course. No one can dispute that what each of these actors did in preparing for their roles was impressive – but what does extreme dieting or exercise have to do with acting? The two are entirely unrelated. One has absolutely *nothing* to do with the other.

Don't get me wrong; I'm not saying these people aren't great actors. I am just saying that manipulating their body fat percentage isn't what makes them great actors. It's an indication of their dedication, to be sure, but not their acting ability. If that was all it took, then Jarod Fogel would be the greatest actor in the world. He lost 245lbs for his recurring role in the Subway commercials. Massive physical transformations are impressive, but they are not the answer.

When moviegoers debate an actor's talent, the term that most frequently pops up in conversation is *range*; in other words, the variety of roles that an actor can convincingly portray. It stands to reason that an actor who can play a wide range of different characters must be better than one who can't. It seems self-evident, and I think it is safe to say most people believe it to be true.

Well...if is true, then there can be no doubt that Lon Chaney was the greatest actor of all time. Chaney appeared in over 150 films throughout the silent movie era and was known as, "The Man of a Thousand Faces". His transformations were complete. Often, he was totally unrecognizable on the screen – even by those who knew him well. In terms of range, Chaney was in a class of his own. He still is.

Nevertheless, is it fair to say that Chaney's performances were purely a result of great acting? Or did they owe something to great makeup? It's worth noting that, despite his enormous popularity and three decades in the industry, Chaney never won an Oscar for Best Actor. And when people think of the silent film era today, Chaney's legacy has been all but eclipsed by a man who achieved on-screen immortality playing exactly the same character, over and over again, in almost every movie that he ever made: Charlie Chaplin.

So, maybe range isn't all that it's cracked up to be, either? The truth is, "range" isn't much more than a tool to impress the general public. Many actors have excellent range. It's just that the public never gets a chance to see them use it.

Joan Washington is a dialect coach for the Royal National Theatre, in London. She has worked with actors on a slew of Hollywood productions, including *"Band of Brothers"*, *"Schindler's List"* and two of the *"Star Wars"* movies. I had the pleasure of studying with Joan in the summer of 1993, and it was then that she told me an interesting story about coaching Robert Redford on the set of *"Out of Africa"*. In the movie, Redford portrays Denys Finch Hatton – an Englishman, and an actual historical figure.

As much as I like Robert Redford, I have a hard time imagining him playing an Englishman. However, according to Joan, (who knows a thing or two about accents) Redford's English accent was perfect. In fact, to use her words, it was "absolutely flawless". Joan was so surprised and delighted once she discovered this, that she ran to the producers and literally begged them to let him use it in the film. They refused.

The reason? It would be too strange for the audience. Redford was an American icon. It would be jarring if he spoke with an English accent – regardless of how well he did it. They felt it just wouldn't look right. And besides, people were not paying to see Robert Redford's range, they wanted to see Robert Redford.

Years ago, audiences thought nothing of watching an Englishman portraying an Arab, as Alex Guiness did in "Laurence of Arabia", or an Irish American playing an Asian, as Mickey Rooney did in "Breakfast at Tiffany's". But times have changed. Today's audiences demand authenticity, not range. It isn't just a matter of being politically correct; it's about immersion and suspension of disbelief. We want something closer to reality.

As our world becomes increasingly competitive, it is getting harder and harder for a "Jack of all Trades" to survive. The people who are most in demand in any business today are the specialists. Actors are no exception.

Robert DeNiro plays tough, likable, mobster-types. Al Pacino plays characters tormented by inner angst. Clint Eastwood is the strong, silent, loner. Johnny Depp seems to have a lock on the oddballs. Being typecast is not a bad thing. On the contrary; it means you have a career.

No actor can play every kind of role. And even if you could, nobody would care. As an actor, it isn't important for you to do everything well; it's only important that you do one thing well. Range is overrated.

Ok. So what is great acting, then?

In his autobiography, "The Ragman's Son", Kirk Douglas gives us the answer. He writes about how his wife used to tell him that he was the worst actor she ever saw, because he could never hide anything from her. She could always tell what he was thinking and feeling just by looking at him.

How's that for irony? The qualities that made Kirk Douglas such a lousy actor in real life are the same ones that made him a mega star, and a fantastic actor on the big screen. There you have it.

Great acting is all about real actions and genuine emotions. These tend to flow more readily if you are passionate (like Kirk Douglas was). Once you care about something or someone, all that is left for you to do is be honest.

An actor who never shows emotions in his private life is going to have a tough time showing them in front of a camera. Instead, he will try to fake it – and very few people can do that convincingly. Most of us can spot a faker a mile away. It becomes even easier under the microscope of a camera lens.

Therefore, in order to be sensitive on the screen, it helps to be sensitive in real life. It stands to reason that if you can't do something when a camera isn't pointing at you, then you're not going to be able to do it when it is.

Acting mirrors reality. The closer your character is to the real you, the less acting required – and the more likely you are to get the job. When directors cast people in roles, they want to see as little acting as possible.

Great acting is about drawing from parts of your real personality, and exposing them for all to see. It is about using your imagination to immerse yourself in a make-believe universe. Once you do that, the rest is easy. You just have to be honest, and tell the truth.

TRUTH

"The actor must believe in everything that takes place on the stage – and most of all, in what he himself is doing. And one can only believe in the truth."
- Konstantine Stanislavski

"With any part you play, there is a certain amount of yourself in it. There has to be, otherwise it's just not acting. It's lying."
- Johnny Depp

Stanislavski's system has influenced actor training in the West ever since his work was first translated into English in the 1920's and 30's. Co-founder of the world-renowned Moscow Arts Theatre, Stanislavski is widely regarded as the father of modern, "realistic" acting. Legend has it that his inspiration come from a dog. The story goes like this:

An actor had a dog, and this dog used to attend rehearsals with its master. Since he was a rather lazy dog, when rehearsals began he would stalk off to a corner of the theatre where he would flop down and sleep all day. However, just before rehearsals would finish each evening, the dog would haul himself up and walk over to the exit with his leash in his mouth, ready to be taken home. What amazed Stanislavski was that the dog somehow always knew that the rehearsal was finished several minutes before his master called for him. Every evening, as regular as clockwork, the dog would trot to the exit and wait there patiently. How did he know?

Finally, Stanislavski figured it out. He realized that the dog could hear when the actors finished acting, and began talking in their normal voices again. The difference between the fake "actor voices", and the relaxed, natural voices of the students was, to the dog, as clear as a bell.

This was a huge lesson for Stanislavski, and it needs to be one for you, too. Whenever you rehearse a monologue or a scene at home, a person in the next room should have the impression that you are talking on the phone with someone. It should be your own natural voice that they hear – not some false, booming "actor" voice. Fake voices (like fake actions and emotions) lead to bad acting.

Simple enough, right? But what about actors that use an accent, or affect their voice for a role – like Johnny Depp did for the character of *Jack Sparrow* in "Pirates of the Caribbean"? That certainly wasn't his normal voice…

True. But Johnny Depp is a well-established pro. It is extremely difficult to alter your voice throughout an entire film and have it re-main consistent. As a fledgling actor, you have enough on your plate already without attempting that. Before you learn how to play some other character-type convincingly, you've got to prove to the world (and yourself) that you can play *you* convincingly.

Johnny Depp earned acclaim by essentially playing himself in the hit TV show "21 Jump Street". It was his convincing performance in that program which gave him the confidence to spread his wings, take chances, and experiment in other roles. But the basis of all his roles is still Johnny Depp. He may change his accent, makeup or mannerisms, but those are just surface trappings. The essence of it is his own being. That's how it is with all successful actors. It has to be.

You are the character. One subtle way of reminding yourself of this is to make sure that you always refer to any character you play in the first person, rather than the third. For instance, if I were asked about playing the role of Detective Trotter in "The Mousetrap", I would never say, "My character appears in the second act," or "He appears in the second act". Both of those would be incorrect. Instead, I would say, "I appear in the second act". It is a tiny mental shift, but it is extremely helpful in reminding me that the character and I are one and the same.

In any role you play, it is always you. It might be you in another time, situation or even universe. You might have a different accent, wardrobe and name, but who cares? That is all surface stuff. Deep inside, animating everything is your mind. They are your memories, insecurities and emotions – not some imaginary character's. The audi-ence doesn't have to know that, but you do.

Before anyone is going to pay you to play the role of a character drastically unlike yourself, you are going to have to prove that you can play a character essentially just like yourself. Or, to put it more suc-cinctly, you're going to have be yourself in front of the camera.

Honesty is the essence of all great acting. Tell a lie, and your body will betray you in a hundred ways. It has been estimated that as much as 90% of human communication is non-verbal. We are constantly giving off messages about our thoughts and feelings to those around us. When we are in front of a camera, it is as if we are under a microscope. All of our movements and facial expressions are amplified.

But what if you're in a movie like *Godzilla* and you have to act like the monster is after you? How can you avoid lying then? Everything's generated by computer graphics; *the truth* is that there is no monster!

Well, this is where your imagination comes in to play. Remember my nieces and nephews from the last chapter? I'm sure if I told them a 70-story prehistoric monster was lumbering down the road, they'd have no trouble at all envisioning it and reacting to it as if it were real. Your imagination needs to be strengthened to the point where you can do that just as well as they can. Once you can see it clearly, you won't have to worry about acting. Your body will *react*; truthfully, and of its own accord.

THE POWER OF STILLNESS

"One of the few axioms I work by as an actor is to get the greatest possible effect with the minimum visible effort."
- Richard Burton

"My old drama coach used to say, 'Don't just do something – stand there.' Gary Cooper wasn't afraid to do nothing."
- Clint Eastwood

Richard Burton learned his lesson while filming on the set of "*Cleopatra*", opposite Elizabeth Taylor. There, she accused him of over-acting. Her advice was that he should merely "think", and trust that the camera would capture his thoughts. At first, Burton was furious, but after watching the dailies, he could see that she was right. Afterwards, he always credited her with teaching him how to act in front of the camera.

The next time you watch an old Clint Eastwood western, observe how little he moves when he speaks. Even his facial expressions are sparse. The fact that he shows so little emotion (and plays such similar characters) led many critics to disparagingly describe him as a movie star rather than an actor, throughout most of his early career. But that is unfair. He's a fine actor.

Delivering your lines in a realistic and convincing manner, while remaining relaxed and motionless, isn't as easy as it sounds. Mastering the technique is a mark of greatness. Try it for yourself. The trick is to be still, but not stiff. When you are stiff, it makes you look nervous, uncomfortable or afraid. A relaxed stillness is a mark of supreme confidence.

You may wonder whether a camera or theatre audience can really differentiate between such slight nuances of tension held within your body, but they can. The message is subtle, intuitive, and like most body language – as clear as a bell.

Think about watching two gunfighters in a classic western as they prepare for a showdown. The camera comes in for an extreme close up of each man's face. Sweat trickles down the brow of one. The other seems relaxed and cool. But they are both perfectly still. Their faces have no expression. They don't blink. They don't even appear to breath. And as we watch them, we mimic them. We don't move, blink or breathe either. The tension is at its peak.

We can't go on like that for long or we'll pass out – so something has to happen. Usually, it's an explosion of gunfire that releases the tension in an instant. But imagine what would happen if one of the gunfighters started to shift his body around? As soon as he started to move, he would look weak compared to the other man. You see this in Clint Eastwood movies such as *"The Outlaw Jose Wales"*, when it is necessary to show one gunfighter as stronger than the other via body language. However, if both gunfighters started moving around too much, we in the audience would feel free to move as well. The tension would drop out of the scene. At least one of them (usually the star) must remain still.

As actors, it is our job to recognize that the audience intuitively connects to our body language. Every physical movement that we make, however slight, holds meaning for them.

By keeping still and being relaxed, an actor comes across as confident and strong. By being stiff, an actor looks nervous, self-conscious, or afraid. There are times when we need to be both of those things – depending on the role we are playing. These are subtle nuances, but they make all the difference in the world.

There are countless examples of wonderful actors using stillness to great effect in the movies. Chow Yun-Fat astonished me with his use of it in *"Crouching Tiger, Hidden Dragon"* and *"Curse of the Golden Flower"*. Other examples that leap to mind are Anthony Hopkins as Hannibal Lector, Cate Blanchett as Queen Elizabeth, and Judy Dench in every role I have ever seen her in.

A word of caution: Don't start straining with hidden effort. If you do, you might burst a vital organ or pop your eyeballs out or something. It would be a pity too, because the "hidden effort" that Burton is referring to has nothing whatsoever to do with physical effort of any kind. What he's actually talking about is *importance*.

IMPORTANCE

William Wyler's 1959 version of *"Ben Hur"*, starring Charlton Heston and Stephen Boyd is one of my all-time favorite movies. The widescreen DVD version is terrific, because you get to see screen tests of other actors who auditioned – one of which was Leslie Nielsen, star of *"Police Squad"*, and *"The Naked Gun"*. If you don't want to buy the DVD, do yourself a favor and rent it for an evening. It's a terrific acting lesson.

One scene that you should pay particularly close attention to occurs early in the film. It is the scene where *Ben Hur* reunites with his former childhood friend, *Messala*. The two men meet, embrace and chat for a while. Pretty simple and straightforward, right?

Leslie Neilson had to perform this scene for his audition and you can observe his efforts in the "bonus" section of the DVD.

Now, please understand, I'm not trying to point the finger at or belittle Neilson in any way. Even back then, he was a well-established actor. The object of this exercise is not to criticize him personally, it's to identify what is wrong with his audition, because it's obvious that something is. He's auditioning alongside Cesare Danova, another veteran actor of the day. They are working on the same scene which appears in the final version of the film, but for some reason it all looks contrived, unconvincing and rather silly by comparison. Why? These are two top actors. What's wrong?

For a start, there is no fancy camera work or editing. The lighting is bland and the sets are basic. Neither is there a musical score playing underneath. All of these things make a difference, but there is more to it than that.

If you listen to Charlton Heston's commentary of the film (found under the "Special Features" section), you will find that he gives us the answer.

Heston tells us that even though the scene doesn't seem all that hard to do, it gave them a lot of trouble. Nobody was really happy with it, but no one knew how to fix it either. Wyler spent two long days shooting the scene. Finally, late into the second evening, he called a wrap and announced that they would finish it the next day.

Heston tells us that he went back to his dressing room and took off his makeup. He was just getting out of the shower when Wyler knocked on his door. "Chuck," he said, "We have to talk".

Heston invited him in, poured him a drink and asked what was on his mind. Wyler stated flatly, "You have to be better in this part, Chuck". Heston said, "Ok, what can I do?" "I don't know", Wyler replied. "If I knew I'd tell you and that would be the end of it. But I don't know. I just know you have to be better."

That's pretty tough direction there. What is an actor supposed to do with that? How can you just "be better"? A lot of actors might have shrugged it off, or gotten angry, but Charlton Heston was a pro who set high standards for himself. He knew Wyler had tremendous instincts as a director and if Wyler felt there was a problem – there was a problem. All that night, Heston worried about it, but he couldn't come up with anything. The next morning, they shot it again.

Miraculously, this time Heston *was* better. It is this version of the scene that appears in the final cut of the movie. So what happened? What did he do differently?

Heston says he himself isn't exactly sure, but he thinks he was more focused. I agree. He was more focused, *because it was far more important to him.*

Think about it. After fretting over it all night long, it had to have mattered to Heston so much more the following day. The stakes were higher. The scene had taken on a whole new level of importance in his real life, isn't it therefore understandable that it would also become more important to the characters on the screen?

Go back and watch Leslie Neilson's audition once again, and this time, you should be able to see what's wrong. It just isn't important to him or Cesare Danova. The stakes are low. There is no conflict for them to focus on, so they focus their attentions on themselves. They are both self-conscious. Neilson strikes manly poses for the camera, and Danova forces himself to laugh heartily. These are two actors "acting", and there is nothing interesting or compelling about that.

This is a tough scene. It's really a trap. If you're playing a character that's being chased by a monster, importance is built into the script. After all, your life is on the line! But in a scene where you're meeting a dear old friend from your childhood? Even though there is no conflict or danger at this point in the story, the importance of this moment cannot be taken for granted. It has to be there. Why? Because if it isn't important to the actors, it isn't important to the audience.

We've all experienced moments of heightened excitement and intensity in our lives. These are significant events that stand out in our minds. Search your memory for such an occasion and consider it closely. What were you thinking at the time? Were your senses heightened and alert? Were you acutely aware of your surroundings? These things usually happen in crises situations when fear and adrenaline kick in. Most people try to avoid such uncomfortable circumstances, but not actors. It is our job to seek them out.

One such moment occurred for me in a scene-study class many years ago. The instructor picked seven couples to pair-up and work on a scene. We had about 30 minutes to go off and rehearse before he started calling us back to perform in front of the rest of the class. It so happened that my partner was a stunning, 22 year-old blonde. We were the last to go on.

This was not your typical audience. The class was full of professional actors who weren't easily impressed at the best of times. By the time our turn came around, the class had already sat through half-a-dozen performances of the same scene, and they were getting tired of it. Since my partner and I had had more time than the other groups to prepare, the pressure was on us to perform.

Unfortunately, I was a mess. I was so enamored by the beauty of my scene partner during our rehearsal together, that I had found it all but impossible to focus on my script. As we stepped onto the stage, I had a strong sense of impending doom. I barely knew my lines.

Looking back now, I can't even remember what the scene was

about. I'm pretty sure that it was just a bunch of meaningless dialogue lumped together, out of which we were expected to come up with something brilliant. In the end, it didn't matter. After we each delivered our opening lines, my partner thrust out her sexy hip and winked at me in a very flirty fashion. That was all it took. I was finished. I lost all focus and completely forgot my next line.

I entered panic mode. The room spun around so I sat in the closest chair. I could see that my partner was waiting for me to speak. I desperately wanted to, but I had nothing. I was literally speechless. I searched her eyes for help, hoping that she would say something – anything. But by that point, she seemed as lost and helpless as I was. I can only assume that she had forgotten her lines too.

Our silence continued for what seemed like an eternity. What made things worse was that a few people in the audience began to laugh. I was aware of it in the back of my mind, but only vaguely. All of the focus and energy of my entire being was going into trying to remember that stupid line. I felt like an idiot. Here I was, after working so hard to build up a good reputation as an actor – humiliating myself in front of my peers. I could hear their laughter intensifying. I was in hell. As a matter of fact, I think I actually started to sweat. At last, mercifully, the line came to me in a flash. I looked up at my partner and said it.

I don't think it would be an exaggeration to say that the audience went completely bananas. They absolutely lost it. Some fell out of their chairs and rolled into the aisles. Others leaned on each other, clutched their sides and howled in pain. I was stunned. We never even finished the scene. The instructor bounded up onto the stage with tears of joy streaming down his face, and hugged me. It was a while before everybody calmed down.

We spent the rest of the class talking about it. No one could understand how a scene that they had already watched half-a-dozen times could suddenly be so hilarious.

They raved about how tormented I had looked upon hearing my "girlfriend's" declaration. They marveled at how genuinely confused and frustrated I had appeared. One fellow went on about how he could see me reliving our entire relationship in my mind. They were astonished at how much more convincing I was compared to the actors who had come earlier. They praised me for my comic instincts, timing, and delivery.

Finally, the instructor placed his hand on my shoulder, and held the other up for quiet. His explanation for what took place is something that I have never forgotten.

He told the class that I was a brilliant actor. Furthermore, he told them that it was something that most of them should never even attempt to do. "It takes incredible confidence," he said, "to be able to remain silent for so long, and yet still keep your thoughts so active, focused and alive." I still remember all the faces looking at me in admiration.

Throughout all of this praise and hullabaloo, I kept my mouth shut. After all, what could I say? The general consensus was that I was a genius – so I just them believe it. The truth of course, was that anybody could have done it. It was simply a matter of not giving up on the scene.

The mental effort that the audience saw wasn't acting at all. It was real. The audience watched me squirm and assumed that my discomfort was related to what was happening in the scene. Only one man said he thought that I had forgotten my line, but then, when he saw what I was doing, he decided that the long pause must have been a conscious choice that I had made.

It wasn't a choice. But it just goes to show how things can turn out if you don't give up on a scene. Everything becomes important. And when a scene becomes important, it is compelling.

TRANSITIONS

Another innocent byproduct of my incompetence was that I stumbled upon a very nice transition. A transition is that part of a scene where something (usually related to the relationship) changes. There should be at least one good transition in every scene. Often there are several. Your value as an actor has a lot to do with the quality and number of your transitions.

Of course, I never planned to have a transition, it just happened. The very best transitions are often surprises. Unfortunately, you can't always rely on them to pop up on their own. You should plan to make at least one transition in every scene. However, you should also be open to allowing them to occur spontaneously and naturally.

Is there such a thing as a scene without any transitions? Sure there is. Usually this is because the scene exists purely to impart information, or because it has been badly written, or both. A scene without transitions is probably a scene that could be cut without anyone really missing it.

There is a scene in the movie, "Pretty Woman", where Edward (played by Richard Gere) presents a fabulous necklace to Vivian (Julia Roberts) before taking her to the opera. The scene has Edward opening a jewelry box and Vivian gazing at a necklace in wide-eyed amazement.

That is not as easy as it sounds. There is a big difference between trying to *act* surprised and actually *being* surprised – especially when you already know what's coming. Again, if you lie about and try to fake it, the camera will expose you as a fraud.

After several takes, director Garry Marshall knew the scene wasn't working, so he came up with a plan. Pulling Richard Gere aside, he asked him to snap the box shut on Julia Robert's fingers in the next take. Gere did as he was told, and the result was movie magic. Julia gasped in shock, snatched back her hand, and laughed.

It was an honest, natural transition, and one of the most delightful moments in the film.

LISTENING

When we are having a conversation in real life, we don't know what our next line is going to be. It all depends on what the other person says. We have to listen to their words, process the information, and think about how we want to respond. Only then do we speak. Of course, all of that can happen in a fraction of a second, but it happens nonetheless. It has to be that way when we're performing too.

Too many actors stand around waiting for the cue to deliver their line. They have no idea what the other person is saying, because they're not listening to them. The only thing they are concentrating on is their next line. They do this because they want to make sure they deliver their line correctly and at precisely the right moment. This is the epitome of bad acting.

Great acting isn't really about saying the lines at all. You don't have to be an actor in order to recite lines. Hell, you don't even have to be a human being. Parrots can do it perfectly well. Great acting is all about what you do *between* the lines.

Do you listen to what the other person is saying? Do you process the information you hear? Do you consider your response? You must do all those things. Occasionally, (as I accidentally discovered) it's ok to take your time with it too! Of course, you wouldn't want to do that with every line, but there's nothing wrong with it once in a while. And if you forget a line completely – so what? People get stumped in real life every day. Roll with it. That's what acting is all about.

Jimmy Stewart was once asked why he always stammered so much, and he said it was usually because he was trying to remember his next line. Watch Stewart in any movie he was ever in and you will see him listening to the other actor as though he is hearing their words for the first time in his life. He focuses on the other person's lines, rather than his own. The result was that his acting always appeared honest and real.

You must listen to the other person and concentrate on what they're saying – rather than on what you're about to say. React to what they are actually saying and doing – not what the script says they're supposed to be saying and doing. Be open to throwing all of your preparations away and allowing the scene develop organically. If you do this, you will find that amazing things happen. You will no longer be concerned about how you're standing or what you're doing with your hands. You will be focused entirely on the other person, the object of your discussion, your goal – any number of things, but not on yourself. Your body will act of its own volition. You will move (or remain still), naturally, and instinctively.

Try to keep these points in mind as you observe other actors on the stage and screen. Watch the great ones whenever you can and pay close attention to their economy of motion, and the way they keep still at crucial moments. Notice how they raise the level of importance in their scenes. Keep an eye out for transitions too. They are often subtle.

You can learn a lot from watching the "not-so-great" actors as well. Judge them by the same criteria as "the greats", and think about how you would improve upon their performances. Finally, watch people in real life. Some of the best acting lessons come from of observing the world around you.

THEATRE

"I think, by and large, the level of acting is mediocre.
When I go to the theatre, I get so angry, I don't go."

- Uta Hagen

What has happened to the theatre? There was a time when audiences used to flock to it in droves. Now, few theatrical companies can survive without relying heavily upon grants and donations. Even then, actors are often paid little or nothing for their efforts.

For many, it is a labor of love. The stage is the only place where an actor is in complete control of their performance, and no longer at the mercy of the director's shot selection or an editor's cuts. Theatre is *our* domain; which is what makes its decline and fall all the more tragic.

The truth is that theatre has been dying for a long time now. We've gotten so used to it squeaking by on artificial life support, few can remember it any other way. Where did it all go wrong?

In my opinion, it happened when people stopped throwing rotten fruit.

In Shakespeare's day, poor performances simply weren't tolerated. When they happened, bad actors were pelted with fruit and vegetables. As it turns out, this wasn't such a bad idea. Either the audience saw a great play, or they had a blast taking part in a massive food fight. Either way, they got their money's worth.

It worked surprisingly well for the actors, too. The threat of being smacked upside the head with a rotten cabbage is an excellent incentive to concentrate. I can't think of anything that would motivate me more.

And for the poor unfortunates who were constantly bombarded (hence the term "bombed" when describing an awful performance) well, I'm sure it didn't take long for most to conclude that they weren't cut out to be actors. No doubt many went on to become successful haberdashers or cobblers. Better for them. Better for society in general.

The problem with theatre today is that there isn't any reason for the bad actors to quit. No one ever throws anything at them but encouragement. No matter how awful they are – the audience always applauds.

Have you ever been to a play where the audience *didn't* applaud? I've seen a lot of terrible shows in my time. I have been in my fair share, too. But no matter how bad the performance, the audience always claps at the curtain call; *every single time*. Why do they insist on doing that?

For one thing, it has become traditional. Also (as previously discussed), most don't know much about acting. Few people go to plays regularly, so it's difficult for them to properly assess a performance. The average theatergoer leaves a play saying the same thing, "How do they remember all those lines?" That's all it takes to impress most people. The quality of the acting is irrelevant.

Peer pressure plays its part as well. Of all the horrendous productions I have had the misfortune of attending, one stands out above the rest. I won't go into details here, because I don't want to embarrass anyone who may have been involved with it. Suffice to say, it was pretty dreadful. When the show mercifully ended and the actors turned out for their curtain call, I was determined not to clap. But I did it anyway – right along with everybody else. I just couldn't help myself.

I love the theatre – really, I do. I just don't like what it's becoming. It reminds me of the children's story of "The Emperor's New Clothes". All too often, people praise a play, simply because they are too embarrassed to admit that they didn't enjoy it, or couldn't understand it. But why should they feel that way? They have paid good money. They deserve to be entertained!

Polite ovations and niceties aren't doing anyone any favors in the long run – least of all the actors. How can they know how effective (or ineffective) they are, if the audience insists on applauding for every performer, at every performance? On the other hand, how can we expect a theatrical audience to be discerning, if they are not experienced enough to know what quality acting looks like? This is the dilemma.

Short of going back to throwing rotten fruit, I don't see how we are ever going fix the situation. Fortunately, that is not our main concern. If we cannot change the way things are, we can at least accept the situation and try to make it work in our favor. Regional community theatre is a great place to start your acting career for a number of reasons:

- *Convenience* – Small, local theatres are just about everywhere.

- *Connections* – It's a great way to meet people in the industry and make lifelong friends.

- *Confidence* – It might be scary at first, but there's no better way to build your confidence. You can learn a lot performing in front of a live audience.

- *Lack of Competition*- The level of the acting will not be high, so you shouldn't have much trouble getting cast. It should also be relatively easy to stand-out in the performance.

- *Fulfillment* – Theatre is a lot of fun. You may find that you love it so much you don't even care that you're not making any money.

- *Visibility* – Theatre puts you in the public eye, and you never know who might be watching.

Another great thing about community theatre is that you don't need an agent to get started. Check your local papers, search online or ask around to find out when the next auditions are being held. All you need is a headshot and a couple of monologues.

Of course, there are downsides to community theatre, as well. There's a significant time-commitment involved, and little or no pay. You'll be working with non-professionals for the most part, so there is a very real possibility that you will encounter bad direction. Hopefully, this book will arm you with the information you need to recognize these situations and handle them accordingly.

Of all the bad direction that a stage actor can receive, by far the worst is the insistence that actors over-project their voice and be "big" in all of their physical movements and reactions. The reasoning here is that if the actor doesn't speak in an unnaturally loud tone and use outrageous facial expressions and gestures, the audience "won't be able to see or hear them." This nonsense has ruined more actors than it is possible to shake a stick at. If you ever hear such direction, you must immediately recognize that you are dealing with someone who has no idea what they're doing.

Remember the dog in Stanislavsky's theatre? *Use your natural voice.* Discarding that fake, over-projected "stage voice" in favor of your own is appreciated by all good theatrical directors. However, bad directors can sometimes put up stiff resistance. Don't worry too much about butting heads with these guys. They are going nowhere fast.

Many years ago, I performed in a small production opposite an incredibly talented young actress named Jodi Marks. Jodi was completely new to acting at the time, but had nevertheless been cast as the leading lady. I remember her being very relaxed on the stage and delivering all of her lines in her own, perfectly natural voice – unlike most of the other actors.

Almost as soon as rehearsals began, there were difficulties. The director became increasingly concerned with Jodi's performance. The natural qualities that he had loved so much in her audition now seemed out-of-place alongside the other cast members who were, for the most part, shamelessly over-acting.

I did my best to use my natural voice as well, but the director never gave me a hard time about it. Perhaps he had more faith in me, because I had more experience. In any event, his confidence in Jodi rapidly declined. He couldn't put his finger on what was bothering him, either. I remember him asking me at one point if I thought she lacked stage presence. I assured him that she had wonderful stage presence (whatever the hell that means), but he remained unconvinced.

Finally, it all came to a head during one rehearsal. He had the cast spread throughout the theatre and made Jodi walk back and forth across the stage, reciting her lines with as much volume as she could manage. No matter how loud she spoke, he insisted that it wasn't loud enough. He had succeeded in convincing himself that she couldn't "project" properly. I sat in the back row and heard every word that Jodi said, as clear as a bell. The problem was all in his mind.

After about thirty minutes of this torture, Jodi lost her voice, and her marvelous self-confidence was shattered. She began to doubt whether she had any acting ability at all, and even seriously considered dropping out of the play. That is the sort of damage a bad director can inflict.

Jodi asked for my opinion on the matter, and I told her that I thought she should play dumb. I advised her to listen to the director with regards to blocking instructions (where to stand, sit, walk, etc...), but that was all. If he gave her line-readings, she was to nod as if she understood, but then ignore them completely. Jodi was skeptical, but desperate. She agreed to give it a shot.

It worked. The director soon tired of beating his head against the wall, and resigned himself to the belief that Jodi was a lost cause. Convinced that she could neither act nor take direction, and that all efforts to teach her otherwise were in vain, he finally left her in peace.

When the play opened, Jodi was a smashing success. As a matter of fact, two talent agencies offered to represent her immediately. Within a year, she was hosting her own television series, "Fix It Up", on HGTV. She went on to be the host of several other of her own shows, including "Southern Home By Design", and she has enjoyed a successful acting career ever since.

Never let anyone talk you into bad acting. By "bad acting", I am referring to movements, facial expressions, or voices that are "fake", "big", "over-the-top" or in any way larger-than-life. I can assure you that sooner or later, someone is going to try to get you to do this sort of thing – especially if you work in community theatre. Don't let them.

You have to be diplomatic about it (we don't want to make enemies if we don't have to), but at the same time you must remain strong and stick to your principles. It is your reputation on the line, after all. If you act badly, you are the one the critics will blame – not the director.

I'm not saying that you should automatically discount what a director tells you. Far from it! I'm just saying that when the direction is bad, you need to have the courage to do the right thing. When you receive criticism, resist the immediate and natural impulse to fight back. Stay humble and try to look at the situation objectively. Occasionally, you may have to translate the message.

Sometimes a director who wants "more", or insists that you need to be "bigger", instinctively understands something is missing from your performance. It might be tempting to write such an opinion off as amateurish – but don't be too hasty. After all, they might be right.

The problem is that even when they know something is wrong, few directors can articulate what it is that's bothering them. Usually, you will have to bridge the gap and figure it out for yourself. As we saw in the last chapter with Charlton Heston in the movie "Ben Hur", often, the missing ingredient is *importance.*

In every scene, there is going to be something that your character wants (If they didn't want anything, they wouldn't speak). Figure out what it is that you want (hint: It's nearly always love) and make that objective a matter of life and death. Then, fight like hell for it.

By adding life and death importance to your performance, your voice will become louder *naturally* in your struggle to communicate. This is the only way to be "bigger" on stage without over-acting.

WHEN IT ALL GOES WRONG

Al Pacino once famously said that working in film and theatre are similar in that both are like walking along a tightrope. The difference is that in film, the rope is lying on the ground, while in theatre it's 100 feet up in the air. That is probably true for Al Pacino, but here again, it is the opposite for you and me.

Pacino can screw-up as much as he likes on the set of a movie, and nobody is going to say a word to him about it. If Al needs 20 takes to get it right, then Al can have his 20 takes. Would you or I get the same consideration? Absolutely not! We had better get it right the first time.

On the stage it's a different story. If you or I blow our lines, or throw the play into disarray with some colossal blunder, odds are, only our fellow performers will ever know the truth. More often than not, the audience will have no idea that anything even went wrong. If Al Pacino blows his lines – *everybody* knows. That's the price of fame. When stars fall on their faces, they do it in front of the world.

Things go wrong in theatre all the time. I've had "wardrobe mal-functions", forgotten my lines, sat on furniture that collapsed underneath me and had scenery fall down around my ears. Several times I've had to fire a gun at someone (or had one fired at me) and the damned thing wouldn't go off. Telephones ring when they shouldn't and don't ring when they should. I was once in a scene with an elderly actress who fell off the stage in the middle of our performance (she was fine, but I was a mess).

Murphy's Law is alive and well in the theatre. If something can go wrong, it probably will. But in every case, no matter what happens, the show must go on. It's all part of the fun. It's also great practice. It teaches you to "live in the moment" and not give up on a scene.

Never give up on a scene. The very best moments happen when an actor goes up on their lines. Invariably, even a dull scene suddenly springs to life. Promise yourself that you will never call out for a line, or stop a scene and start over again – especially in auditions. No matter what happens, stick with it and see where it goes. That is the ride that you are signing up for as an actor.

Usually, everybody is nervous about opening night, but the real danger comes when people start to relax after the first few performances. Once they have gotten some shows under their belts, actors tend to slip into auto-pilot mode. That's when lines get dropped and things start to go wrong. If we were acting in Shakespeare's time, this is when you would expect the rotten fruit to start flying. Be on your guard and stay alert.

- Notice what's happening around you on stage. If something out of the ordinary occurs – don't ignore it. *React to it.*

- Never fall into the habit of anticipating another actor's lines. You don't know how they're going to deliver them, or even if they're going to remember to say them at all.

- Don't assume you know how the scene, or play, is going to end. You really don't.

• Realize and accept that absolutely anything can happen on the stage at any given time. That way, you won't be thrown for a loop when it does.

Follow these basic guidelines and you will be better than 90% of the actors in most community and local theatre productions. You might even be better than many of the actors in the equity playhouses. Compared to the fake, stilted, and artificial performances that are so commonplace in the theatre today, you should be far more realistic and compelling to watch.

Regardless of how large or small your part is, there is a good chance that you will steal the show. This is how you begin to make a name for yourself. It isn't that difficult. In fact, it's a lot of fun! Believe in yourself and do good work. It won't go unnoticed.

SELF-ASSESSMENT

"When you are tough on yourself, life is going to be infinitely easier on you".

- Zig Ziglar

Not everyone is cut out to be a professional actor. The purpose of this book isn't to try and convince you that you can make a living in this business, because many of you won't be able to. My goal is to give you enough insight and knowledge so that you can realistically assess your chances, and then maximize them. If you do not have what it takes, I would prefer that you recognize the fact early (and with minimal expense), rather than wasting years of your life pursuing a career where you have little or no chance of success.

Perhaps no more than 20 to 30 percent of the people reading this book have a realistic shot of making a full-time living in this business. 50 to 60 percent might turn it into a decent, part-time living, and the remaining 20% have no chance whatsoever. How can you be sure which category you fall into? By giving it your best shot right out of the gate, and by committing to being your own worst critic.

Back in chapter 2, I talked about what it takes to succeed in this industry. Since you are still reading, I assume you think you possess enough of those qualities to make pursuing this worth your time. It's great that you believe in yourself (and it's vitally important), but you must recognize that ultimately, what you think of your own abilities isn't the real question. In the end, it's what other people think that counts.

One of the most difficult things an actor ever has to do is be objective about themselves. It's almost impossible, really. Who among us can look in a mirror and say that we see ourselves in the same way that everyone else sees us? Perhaps no one on Earth. We are all either too hard, or too easy on ourselves. The same is true of trying to judge our own talent. If we want to assess our abilities accurately, we have no choice but to rely on the judgment and feedback of others.

Most actors understand that. That's why they're always asking for opinions on their performances. They're concerned about what others think, and they want as much positive feedback and encouragement as possible. Indeed, they depend upon it. It's completely understandable. But it's also a terrible mistake.

The problem is, while everyone is certainly entitled to their opinion, not all opinions have equal value. Some are informed and educated – others are not. In other words, even though your family and friends may have thought you were wonderful in a performance, you would be wise to take their comments with a grain of salt.

In fact, the opinions of family and friends should be discounted entirely – at least when it comes to assessing your true talent and potential. That's because it is all but impossible for them to remain objective. They are too close to you in real life. The only opinions that really concern us are those that are objective, informed, and *unsolicited.*

Why unsolicited? Because when you ask someone for their opinion, you are putting them on the spot. Nine times out of ten, they're going to say, *"You were wonderful!"* whether or not you actually were. What good is that going to do you? How will it help you assess your true value? Soliciting opinions is really nothing more than fishing for cheap compliments. It might give your ego a nice little temporary boost, but in the long run, that could do you more harm than good.

It is this sort of unearned (and undeserved) false-positive feedback that keeps so many actors hanging-on in this business when, in reality, they never had any real chance of succeeding on even the most basic level. Self-delusion is the very thing we are trying to avoid. It leads to wasted lives.

Do the opinions of critics count? For the most part, no, they don't. Most critics are neither objective, nor informed. Few have ever worked as an actor, taken an acting class, or directed anything in their lives. There's no aptitude test that critics need to pass in order to prove their competence. Most are just ordinary people paid to write an opinion and make it sound interesting. All of the great actors have been lambasted by critics at some point in their careers – which only goes to show that critics shouldn't be taken too seriously.

For our purposes, the opinions that count most are those of the people who hire actors. When these individuals hand you a compliment, you can take it to the bank. The comments of working actors, agents, managers, directors and other *working* industry professionals are also of value to you. Just take care that you don't go fishing for them.

What if you are doing a lot of acting in the classroom, local theatre, and/or auditioning regularly, but no one is giving you any unsolicited feedback on your work?

This is a red flag. You must understand that people in this industry are very vocal when they come across someone with genuine talent or potential. If no-one is coming up to you and telling you how good you are, you need to take that into serious consideration. It can only mean one of three things:

1. You are talented, but the people around you do not recognize it. This is certainly possible, although unlikely. If it is true, you need to move somewhere else.

2. You have average ability. This is usually the case, and it isn't good news. It's tough to make a living as an actor when you are mediocre. However, this isn't necessarily a deal-breaker, either. It may be that you have more work to do before things click into place. Or you might need to move to a different region where you are more in demand. Either way, it's probably worth sticking with acting for a while longer. Even in the worst-case scenario, you could still be able to earn decent money doing it part-time.

3. You're just not good – and nobody's telling you the truth because they don't want to hurt your feelings. Keep in mind that this is going to be true for perhaps 20% of the people reading this book.

No matter how you look at it, if you are not receiving objective, informed and unsolicited compliments on your work, you need to take a hard look at your current situation and/or choice of career.

True confidence comes from *knowing* that you are good at what you do. Believing in yourself, having faith in yourself, trusting in yourself – these things are important, but they aren't enough. Others must have faith in you too. You have to give them a reason to believe. You have to prove to them that you deserve it. You will know when you do that, because they will not hesitate to tell you.

Another thing you need to ask yourself is, "Am I having fun?" Perhaps the answer to this question trumps all others. If you're having a great time, and you're excited and fulfilled by what you're doing – who cares about the money? You can always do something else for a living. What matters is that you have found something in life that you're passionate about. That is a major success story in itself.

Even if all indications seem to point to the fact that you have medi-ocre talent, there's still hope if you truly love what you're doing. With time and effort, you can almost certainly become good. You should be under no illusions however, because it will take you time and effort. You can't just sit around waiting to be discovered.

Start with an assessment of where you stand. Pull out a pencil and a piece of paper. Draw two columns on the paper and at the top of each write *STRENGTH* and *WEAKNESS*.

What are your strengths and weaknesses? Start with your physical attributes. Begin at the top of your head and work your way down. Be brutally honest.

How is your hair? Do you consider it to be one of your strengths? There is no middle ground here. It goes in one column or the other. Continue until you have covered the length of your body, then go back through and consider what you can do to turn weaknesses into strengths.

Do you need a better haircut? If you're dying it a certain color – does it *look* dyed? Would you be better off going back to your natural color? You get the idea. Don't just spend your time dwelling on what's wrong either; reinforce the positives. Every step that you take in the right direction brings you one-step closer to your goals.

Men who are losing their hair should know that balding isn't necessarily a weakness. There are a ton of roles for balding men. You can do quite well by filling a particular niche that is in demand. Play to your strengths.

If you are thinking about plastic surgery, I do not recommend it. Actors are often self-conscious about a physical feature that makes them look "different", but these are the very features that could make them marketable.

Consider Steve Buscemi. He's one of the few actors in Hollywood with crooked teeth. Most actors would have rushed to the dentist and had those fixed, but Buscemi was smart enough to realize that they made him unique. They give him a terrific character look, *and he works all the time*. The same can be said for Adrien Brody's large, and rather crooked nose. If you want to stand out as an actor, it helps to look different. Therefore, unless you have a serious deformity, plastic surgery should be considered off-limits for now. The issue you want to fix could turn out to be your money maker.

Similarly, don't worry about your height. In most instances, it's irrelevant on camera. Some stars are tall and many others are short. Unless your height is extreme, it isn't going to be an issue.

While there is nothing that you can do about your height, and I don't recommend doing anything about your face, the shape of your body is entirely up to you. Mold it however you like. There are roles for all body types, but actors who look healthy tend to be the ones who work more often. The easiest way to look healthy is to be healthy. There's no magic to it; just eat right and exercise.

Finally, where does reading, imagination, voice and self-confidence fall on your list? Do you even have them listed at all? If any one of those traits is not listed as a strength, then by default, you need to consider it as a weakness. Work on it.

REASSESS

"Every ten years, a man should give himself a good kick in the pants."
- Edward Steichen

None of us is set in stone. Every ten years or so, we move into a different category. This nearly always takes you by surprise and it can be pretty unsettling. I know; I've already been through one such transition in my career and I'm going through another one right now. These are the times when we need to give ourselves, "a good kick in the pants."

A lot of people look good for their age, especially in this business.

I'm in my mid-forties and I'm occasionally told that I could pass for early thirties. However, when I audition against guys who actually are in their early thirties, there's an obvious difference. I look older than they do.

People take better care of themselves now than they did twenty years ago. If you eat right and exercise, you'll almost certainly reach middle age looking younger than your parents did when they got there.

My agent represents one actress in her mid-forties who refuses to audition for any roles over thirty-five. She looks fantastic and compared to her non-actor friends, she probably does look as though she is in her early thirties. But she isn't auditioning against her non-actor friends! She's going up against women who really are ten to fifteen years younger than she is.

Furthermore, these are not average-looking women that you might find hanging around at the local mall. They are professional actresses who look stunning in their own right. If she would just let go of her ego and read for roles in her own age group, she would make a killing. But she won't. Not surprisingly, she rarely ever works.

Actors who lack the courage for honest self-assessment aren't doing themselves any favors in the long run. Unless your friends and family are in the business of hiring actors, their opinions about your talent and appearance don't amount to a hill of beans in terms of your career. All that really counts is what the professionals think. When they give you an opinion, you need to listen.

PERCEPTION

"With my sunglasses on, I'm Jack Nicholson.
Without them, I'm fat and 60."
- Jack Nicholson

"Everybody wants to be Cary Grant. Even I
want to be Cary Grant".
- Cary Grant

Perception is a big part of acting. In fact, you could argue that it's the only thing that really counts. How you're perceived by the audience and the industry will determine not only the extent of your career, but whether or not you ever have one to begin with. The maddening thing is that it's all so subjective.

If you want to be a lawyer, you have to pass the bar in order to prove your competence. To trade securities, you must pass the Series 7 exam. It's the same for nearly every industry in the world. The requirements for admittance may not be easy, but they are at least clear and well-defined. Not so with acting. In this business, competence is a matter of personal opinion; and everyone is entitled to their opinion.

Let's assume that you're a producer and you need to hire someone. You call up an agent, tell her what you're looking for, and she gives you four actors to choose from. For simplicity's sake, I won't bother to give them names, let's just call them actors "A, B, C and D".

Since you're a producer, it's likely that you've never taken an acting class or read a book about acting in your life, so you don't consider yourself to be an expert on the subject. Therefore, you rely on input from agents and casting directors (as well as other factors) to help you make a decision.

In this instance, you don't know anything about these actors at all, and we have yet to hold an audition, so it's impossible for you to tell which one is the best. But watch what happens when we add just one additional piece of information…

Let's say all four actors have standard day-rates (the amount that each charges per day). Actors "A, B and C" cost $500 a day, while "D" costs $800 a day.

Now, based on that information, who would you say is the best actor? Take your time and think about it. Did you pick one? Alright then, be honest, which one did you choose?

If you are like most actors, you will respond (rather cleverly) that we still can't know who the best actor is, since we have yet to see any of them act!

This is perfectly true. However, it is not the answer we are looking for. If that was your answer, then you are thinking like an actor – not a businessperson. That is something you are going to have to change.

Any businessman worth his salt won't hesitate to say that "D" is the best actor – based purely on the information available. They won't even think twice about it. That's because the cardinal rule of business is: *You get what you pay for.* All businessmen are acutely aware of the ability of a free market system to accurately assess the value of something. In fact, their entire adult lives have revolved around that very concept. To a businessman, it is self-evident that if something costs more, it is worth more. In the corporate world, *more expensive = better.*

That surprises many actors. Some have a tough time accepting it even after I explain it to them a few times. This is because the philosophy of a typical actor is diametrically opposed to the corporate way of thinking. Actors reason that since theirs is an inconsistent business, they must pinch every penny and hunt for bargains wherever they can find them. That's why, in the typical actor's world, *less expensive = better.*

I'm not saying businessmen aren't interested in a bargain price. They are. But they aren't nearly as price-averse as the majority of actors. If I had phrased the original question in a slightly different way and made one of the choices significantly less expensive than the other three, most actors would assume that a businessman would immediately zero in on the least expensive actor as being the most desirable. And they would expect that actor to be the one most likely to get the job. They would be wrong.

Successful businessmen are usually savvy enough to realize that a cheap product is priced that way for a reason. The truth is, when a businessman sees anything marked substantially below normal market value, their initial reaction is usually, "What's the catch?"

I'm not berating actors for being frugal. I'm pretty frugal myself. But it is vital for actors to realize that a higher price tag is not the deal-breaker in a negotiation that most imagine it to be. On the contrary, a higher price tag often has the *opposite* effect. It can make them want you more.

The very first paid acting job that I ever had was for a live corporate event. A producer was hiring actors to play several scenarios for a presentation to employees for entertainment and educational purposes. They had asked an actor buddy of mine to play the role first, but since he had a conflict and couldn't make it, he passed my name along to the producer instead.

The role was tiny. I think I only had a couple of lines. The actor who was playing the lead was well-established and highly respected around town. He also had a ton of dialogue to deliver. I knew from my friend that the lead was being paid $350 for his performance, and that the producer was considering several other actors for my part.

Since it was all happening last minute, there was no time for auditions. I was pretty sure that the other actors would ask for something in the neighborhood of $250 for the day, so I asked for $450. Guess who got the job? I did.

Now remember, this was my first paying gig, I was a complete novice. Yet the producer was happy to pay me substantially more than he was paying the lead. As an actor, you might think that doesn't make any sense at all – but it does to a producer.

Put yourself in his shoes: You're responsible for putting together a convention that is going to cost the company tens of thousands of dollars. You only have so much money to devote to the talent (typically, 3% of the budget). The pressure is on you to make the show successful, so you need to go out and get the best actors you can find with the money you have.

The problem is that you're a producer, not an actor, and you really don't know the first thing about acting. So you ask around and look for recommendations. Since you are no judge of acting-ability, you search for something more tangible; something you can understand. You look for *credibility*.

An actor with credibility is an actor that you can trust. But how to judge an actor's credibility? For most businessmen (and for this one in particular) you judge it the old fashioned way – by how much he costs.

Think about the sayings that corporate people live by: "It takes money to make money"; "Money talks and bullshit walks"; "You get what you pay for." This is how businesspeople think. Money is not just something you use to buy things with; it is a tool for measuring value.

By charging a higher rate than my competitors, I separated myself from the other actors and gained instant credibility in the producer's eyes. He didn't need to audition us to know who the best actor was. He did what most businessmen in his shoes will always do: he assumed that the most expensive actor had to be the best.

The funny thing is that most actors in this sort of situation will lower their rate in an effort to make themselves look more attractive to the producer. It never seems to occur to them that by reducing their rate, they are undermining their own cause. A successful acting career hinges on building your value – not lowering it.

Remember, most of the people who hire actors are not great judges of talent, so they will usually fall back to assessing what they can understand – credibility. The best actor may or may not win the role. The most credible actor nearly always does. Which brings us to…

MAJOR CREDIBILITY INDICATORS:

Cost: More expensive = more credible.

Experience: Both quality and quantity matter.

Reputation: A good rep is tough to beat; a bad one, tough to shake.

Self-confidence: If you don't believe in you, who will?

Schedule: Good actors are busy. Bad ones are always ready and available.

Desperation: The kiss of death. Nobody hires a starving actor.

Quality of work: Difficult for many in the industry to assess.

Training: Only nationally recognized programs count
                       towards credibility. Everything else is fluff.

Appearance: Do you look successful? If you expect them to
                       believe you are worth big bucks, you had better
                       look the part.

Most of these are self-evident if you think about it. Unfortunately, the majority of actors don't think about it. Most focus on developing their acting skills to the exclusion of all other things. If you understand the concept of credibility and how can be used in your favor, you will have a distinct advantage over them.

Imagine waiting to audition for a commercial. The actors all around you are nervous. Some are chatting with each other, others are practicing their lines. How great would it be to look around that room at all of your competitors, and know in your heart that you have already won the role before the audition even takes place?

It's entirely possible. In fact, I have done it many times. The secret is to have your agent make it clear to the casting director and/or the client ahead of time that you are more expensive than everybody else. It has to be made clear to them up front, before you ever walk in the door. If they know you are more expensive ahead of time, there is a chance that they won't want to see you. Usually, however, they will want to see you, even if it's only for the sake of comparison.

When that happens, you can be pretty sure that they consider you to be the best actor before you ever step in the room. If they have agreed to see you, that means they have already decided that they have the extra money to spend, and they are willing to spend it – now they just want to see if you are worth it. In other words, the job is now yours to lose. The only way you can lose it is by completely blowing the audition (which shouldn't happen), or by having someone else upstage you by giving a truly mind-blowing performance. Baring either of those two events, the job is yours; and if the worst happens and one of those things does occur…well, you wouldn't have gotten the role anyway, so what have you really lost?

Being the most expensive actor at an audition gives you instant credibility. This is tough for a lot of actors to accept. Maybe you're having a hard time coming to grips with it now. But, as hard as it might be for you to believe, this is the way it works.

The money that producers and ad agencies spend on an actor doesn't come from their own personal paychecks; it is a corporate expense. What's more, this is money that they have already decided to spend. The only question they have to answer now is, "who do we hire?" Obviously, a producer who answers that question with, "The cheapest possible actor" isn't going to stay in business very long.

Imagine you are out shopping for a car. Is your only requirement going to be the cheapest possible car? If you're living under a bridge and eating at soup kitchens, then yes, price will probably be your only concern. But as your income level rises, other requirements will start to come into play. In no particular order, these might be things such as dependability, performance, practicality, looks, fun-factor and prestige.

Is $10,000 too much money to spend on a car? Maybe. Maybe not. It depends on what kind of car we're talking about. If it's a rusted old beater that barely runs, then yes, it's too much to spend. But if it's a two-year-old Aston Martin, it's the bargain of the century. Money isn't the real issue; *value* for money is.

It is exactly the same for producers and directors who are out "shopping" for actors. Money will always be one of their concerns, but it will never be the only one (regardless of what they try to tell you and your agent when negotiating your rate). The only exception is when you're dealing with a production that is teetering on the verge of bankruptcy, and in such a case, you're probably better off avoiding them altogether anyway. The issue of whether or not to hire you will never really be about how much you *cost*; it will always be about how much you are *worth*.

Years ago, I was talking to an ad agent and a producer about the cost of hiring movie stars. The producer mentioned that UPS had approached Tom Selleck about doing radio commercials for them. Apparently, even though he was relatively new to the voice over industry at the time, Mr. Selleck's going rate was $1 million per commercial. Upon hearing of this staggering price-tag, the ad agent's reply was very interesting. She simply shrugged and said, "Well…he must be worth it."

This is just one more real-life example of what I'm talking about. When they hear your staggering price tag, you should realize that their first reaction is nearly always going to be the same. Just make sure you don't give them a reason to be disappointed in your work, and they won't be. It's all about perception.

Jim Carrey was a moderately successful stand-up comic before he landed a role on the hit television show, "In Living Color". From there, he made the leap to feature films. It wasn't long after that that he began earning serious money. With "Ace Ventura: Pet Detective", Carrey broke the $20 million salary mark; making him by far the most expensive actor in the world at that time.

But was he the best actor in the world? Few would argue that he was. In fact, I doubt even Jim Carrey would ever claim such a thing. He had never been formally trained as an actor, and yet there he was standing all alone at the top of the mountain.

Of course, he didn't stay there for long. Other savvy Hollywood stars such as Arnold Schwarzenegger and Mel Gibson were quick to plant their flags in the sand and demand higher paychecks for themselves. Proving once again that the top actors (and agents) know all about this credibility game and how it should be played.

But these are Hollywood big-shots. How does any of this relate to you, the actor who is just getting started? Obviously, you can't just walk into an agent's office and demand to be the highest paid actor in the city when you have no resume and no experience. That would be totally ridiculous, wouldn't it? Well...don't be so sure.

When I first started acting, I had a lot of auditions, but couldn't seem to book any jobs. I kept getting callbacks ("Callbacks", if you don't already know, are when you are called-back for another round of auditions), but I always seemed to come up short in the end. It was frustrating. There were many times that I felt I was better than the person I was reading against. What was the problem?

Since I had come from a sales background, I knew the importance of credibility and I knew that I had a problem with it. There was no question that my resume was much weaker than most, and I reasoned that it could be a major stumbling block for anyone considering hiring me. However, other than lying about my acting experience, what could I do? I called my agent and set up a meeting.

Decked out in my best suit and tie, I arrived promptly and wasted no time in getting to the point. With a straight face and in my most serious, businesslike manner, I informed her that I wanted to raise my rates to 30% more than what the other actors were getting. She thought I was joking. But I wasn't.

I justified my position by saying that even though I realized I hadn't worked nearly as much as the actors I was reading against, I had observed my competitors in the auditions on many occasions. I knew that I was better.

I explained to her my theory that my resume, and not my acting ability, was the reason I wasn't booking jobs. The decision makers were hesitant to pull-the-trigger on an actor with such a meager background history. If, however, I were priced according to the level of my ability, and not my work history, they would feel safer in selecting me.

I also pointed to my consistent record of callbacks as proof that I was not just another self-deluded actor, but a top-level talent. I delivered this presentation with the same confidence and authority that I would have used in any presentation in the business world. The result? No sale.

My agent wasn't buying. She told me that she thought I was a promising young actor, but that I needed more experience (Translation: A bigger resume – duh!). In her opinion, I still needed to put my dues in. I didn't like this decision, but having made my case, there wasn't much left for me to say. I thanked her for her time, agreed to abide by her better judgment, and walked away.

So this was a total failure, right? Well, you could easily be forgiven for seeing it that way. In fact, I'm sure I felt I had failed at the time. However, I was wrong in that assessment. It was a smashing success.

I know that now, because a few years ago, this same agent reminded me about our conversation. She told me that I made quite an impression on her at the time, and it was then that she realized I was unlike most of the other actors she represented. From that day forward I was, in her words, "a true pro".

After that day, I was at the forefront of her mind. When speaking to producers, she tended to pitch them in the same way I had pitched her. She addressed my lack of experience with them, and told them not to worry about it, because I was good. She probably didn't knowingly go out of her way to give me any special treatment; she just did it because she really believed it. In truth, she had never even seen me act!

So what did I accomplish? By simply attempting to raise my rates, I proved to my agent that I was confident in my acting ability, that I was not desperate for work (since I was willing to walk away from lower paying jobs), and that my appearance was polished and professional. That's three strong credibility indicators. I also addressed my weakest link (experience) head on. Not bad for one meeting.

It is important to understand that I wasn't trying to "pitch" or "con" her in any way. I sincerely believed what I was saying. In essence, I gave a monologue in her office. It was probably better than any stage monologue I could have ever delivered, because it was personal, spontaneous, and from the heart. Whether or not my opinion of my own talent was accurate is beside the point. The vital fact is that I believed in myself; so much so, that I was able to make an impression upon her.

Perhaps you aren't ready to raise your rates yet. Maybe you lack the experience or self-confidence. That's fine. What is most important is that you are honest with yourself. For now, concentrate on improving your skills and standing out from the competition. Raising your rates is going to be a vital step in your future success, and reaching that point is a major milestone in your career that you should always be working towards.

However, until you reach that point, what can you do in the meantime? Well, you can start turning down auditions. To many actors, this is even more unthinkable than raising their rates! But turning down auditions can build your credibility almost as fast as booking jobs can.

Let's look at another hypothetical situation. This time, imagine that you are a talent agent. A casting director calls up and wants you to submit actors for a commercial audition. It is non-union job and will only pay $1000 for a two-year buyout (This might sound like a lot of money to some of you out there, but it is actually a terrible deal). You decide to run it by your actors to see if anyone is up for it.

Actors "A, B and C" jump at the chance, but "D" passes due to the low rate. You let actor "D" know that you admire her for "sticking to her guns", and that, hopefully, some better paying jobs will be coming along soon. A few days later, someone calls the agency looking for movie extras. The rate is $100 per day. Again, all actors go for it, except for actor "D".

The following week, a network commercial is casting. It's a big job, but it comes with a catch: Since so many people will be auditioning, the casting director only wants to see the top three actors from each agency. As a talent agent, you will now have to decide which three to send. Who will be number one on your list? Why, actor "D" of course...

You will do this for a couple of reasons: You have been promising "D" for some time that better work will be coming and now it is here (In other words, you feel a measure of obligation). Second, because the actor has shown patience and self-respect, you can't help but respect her for it. By refusing jobs that others take, actor "D" has, almost by default, become one of your "better actors".

Think about that for a moment. By turning down lousy work, you can succeed in categorizing yourself as one of the top actors at an agency. What's more, if the agent has informed the casting director of your unwillingness to audition for low-paying jobs, the casting director will have more respect for you too. When you finally do make it to one of their auditions, you can be sure they will be watching you closely.

This works well within certain limitations. First of all, when you show up, you had better be good. This is a performance industry, and to succeed in it, you will eventually need to perform. But then, we already knew that, didn't we?

Again, the goal is not to "con" or "fake" your way to the top; it is to build demand for an excellent product: You.

But what if you don't feel excellent? What if you feel that you are just an average actor – not much better or worse than most of the other actors that you see in classes and auditions all the time?

That's a problem. And it brings us to what I like to call, *The Iron Law of Acting Economics*. It goes like this:

> *Actors unable to command above-average wages in a given market are considered by that market to be mediocre. Mediocre actors lack the minimum requirements necessary for sustained, professional success.*

In this business, "average" doesn't cut it. Remember, 95% of SAG actors make less than $7,000 per year. If you don't think you have what it takes to be a top-level talent, then at least be honest with yourself. Either move to another city where your talent will be considered "above average", or accept that for you, acting is never going to be anything more than a part time job, or a hobby. Accept that fact and enjoy it for what it is, or move on with your life and pursue another career.

What if you do believe you have what it takes to be a top-level talent, but you are hesitant to raise your rates for fear of losing out on too many jobs?

This is a valid concern. Remember, you never want to be in a position where you need the job. You should always have savings to fall back on if times are slow. If you don't have savings, then you must generate some. Pick up a part-time job, live within your means, do whatever you have to do. To be successful in this business, it's vital that you have the confidence and ability to walk away from acting jobs. Let me illustrate this with a true story:

Brian is a Los Angeles actor and has been a close friend of mine for many years. Lately, live conventions have played a larger role in his annual acting income. These conventions usually take the form of trade shows for major corporations. Brian's job is to stand up in front of a live audience and deliver the company's "pitch" to the media and other convention attendees. I dread these sorts of shows myself – they're just not my thing. But Brian is relaxed, funny and spontaneous. He's very good at what he does.

I happened to be working on a job in LA when one of the major national banks (I won't mention any names) asked Brian if he would be willing to appear as a spokesperson for them at a summer trade show in Miami. There wasn't much happening for Brian work-wise at the time, so the offer was welcome. There was just one catch: It was a lousy deal.

The company was only willing to pay him $250/day, for four days. He had to buy his own plane ticket, pay for his own hotel, and they weren't going to give him any per diem, either. Presumably, he was also expected to provide for his own transportation to and from the convention.

Brian figured, after subtracting out his costs, he might net around $50 to $80 per day if he stuck to a tight budget and got a cheap hotel. He needed the money, and was seriously considering accepting the deal – until I talked him out of it.

I basically gave him the same speech that I have just given you. I asked him to "pick the best actor – A, B, C or D". I preached to him about the importance of his *value* and *perception* in the business world.

He agreed that my points made sense, but countered with the fact that a lot of the spokespeople he knew would be willing to take the deal. I asked him if he considered himself to be better than most of those guys. "Yes", he said, "I suppose I am." "Well then," I replied, "If you're better than the others, why should you be paid the same as them?"

To his credit, Brian listened, and eventually he agreed to take my advice and reply to the bank's offer with a counter-offer of his own. Actually, I sat down and wrote it for him. It went like this:

Dear _____,

Thanks so much for the offer to represent
_____ at the convention. Currently,
my schedule is open for the show dates.
However, things have been extremely busy for
me ever since moving to Los Angeles and I'm
afraid I wouldn't be able to justify booking out
a full week of my time for anything less than
$850 a day. Naturally, I would also expect the

company to cover my airline and hotel costs – as well as provide me with a reasonable per diem.

I realize this is more than what you have budgeted for, and completely understand if you need to go with someone else. Let me know what you decide. I look forward to hearing from you.

Sincerely,
Brian N.

I should also mention that I advised Brian to tell the bank to contact him via his agency, rather than by emailing him directly. He decided against that, since he thought he might be pushing his luck. He was completely wrong in that assumption (as we shall soon see), but I figured I needed to work him up to speed slowly, so I let it drop.

Notice that the letter is polite, but not overly so. There's no reason to kiss anybody's ass. On the other hand, there's no need to be "snippy" either. We hit them right between the eyes with a big, fat, day-rate up front. Then we stress the busy schedule (major credibility indicator).

What we're really saying is, "Look, I am not some starving actor – I'm a pro. Please don't waste my time with any more offers like this in the future."

Using terms like "naturally" and "reasonable" when referring to the flight, hotel and per diem reinforces the fact that it is standard practice for a production to cover these costs. They know that, and you need to let them know that you know it too. If you find yourself dealing with a new production company that doesn't know any better, then it's up to you (or your agent) to bring them up to speed. Never be afraid to let them know you're a pro.

Finally, we finish off with the gentle statement that this is non-negotiable. If they want a budget actor, they're going to have to go and look somewhere else. We're taking a strong stance here. The ball is now squarely in their court.

Brian was a little nervous at first, but after we sent the email off he began to feel better. He hated the thought of turning down work, especially since it had been so slow for him as of late. He thought it pretty unlikely that they would agree to pay him $850 per day, but he felt there was a good chance that they might counter with $500 a day. He hoped they would also agree to pay for at least some of his expenses. Empowered by the possibilities, his spirits rose.

Only to be dashed the following day. The letter was rejected. There was no counter offer. No money. No job.

I could see that Brian was disappointed. He told me again that he couldn't afford to lose jobs. I tried to put things in perspective for him:

ROY: *"What have you lost?"*

BRIAN: *"$400."*

ROY: *"Maybe $400, assuming you could have kept your costs down and gotten a cheap flight. It would have probably been closer to $250. Also, it's not like that was free money. You were going to have to work pretty hard for it. Now, what have you gained?"*

BRIAN: *"Nothing."*

ROY: *"Not true. You've gained a lot of things."*

BRIAN: *"Such as?"*

ROY: *"The respect of that company, for one. Talk is cheap, but you've just backed up your talk by putting your money where your mouth is. By turning down their offer, you've proven to them that you're a serious actor. They were probably shocked that you charged so much, but you have their attention and respect now. Odds are, they will remember your name. If you think about it, you've just gotten the kind of advertising that money can't buy – and all you had to do to get it was give up a crappy, low-paying job that you never really wanted in the first place."*

BRIAN: *'That's great, but what am I supposed do in the meantime?"*

ROY: *"Something else! That's another valuable thing you've gained: Time. Time is money! You now have a week to work, or to do something else to further your career. Who knows what auditions will come along which you would have missed out on if you were down in Miami? When you total up the costs involved with doing a job, you must include the loss of potential opportunities."*

Fortunately, Brian could see the truth in all of this, so he didn't punch me in the face or anything.

About six weeks later, I was back home when Brian called me with great news. The same bank had contacted him and wanted to hire him for an upcoming trade show in Seattle. This time, they were willing to meet every last one of his requirements: $850/day + all expenses paid. Brian was thrilled.

It gets better. The company was so happy with his performance in Seattle, and so convinced that they now truly had the right man for the job, that they have continued to hire him regularly ever since. Brian now has a regular gig going with a client who treats him very well.

Everyone's happy, and it's all because he was willing to draw a line in the sand, set a minimum standard, and stick to it.

Nobody wants to be ripped off, and no one wants to pay more than they absolutely have to. But when you charge a premium price, and you back it up with premium service – everyone is happy. Most clients are willing to pay more to work with a pro, because it takes stress off of them. They're relieved to know that the talent is one less thing that they have to worry about. It's like paying a little more for insurance. It's a load off their mind.

Brian's story might sound like a fluke, but it isn't at all. I have had countless similar experiences throughout my career.

For instance: An insurance company in Florida wanted to shoot a non-union ad to run on the internet for one year. They were willing to fly the talent down to Tampa, but they were only willing to pay $1000. I agreed to audition for the role, but I had my agent make it clear to them from the beginning that if they chose me, I would cost them a lot more.

It's The Takeaway in action. People want what they can't have. It is human nature. I don't know if I was the best actor at the audition; all I know is that I was the most expensive. You would be shocked how often this simple "price takeaway" works.

Sure enough, within a few days they called my agent and informed her that they wanted to hire me. My agent told me about the telephone conversation afterwards. According to her, the producer said, "Well, we want Roy, but all we can come up with is an additional $3800. Will that be enough?" My agent gave the perfect reply and said, "I'll ask."

It doesn't always work out so well. There have been plenty of times when I've lost out on jobs, but I'm willing to make that trade. Instead of looking at it as a "lost job", I consider it to be free advertising. As long as producers are walking around town saying, "we really wanted to hire Roy McCrerey for this role, but we couldn't afford him." I'm a happy man.

Producers are so used to working with starving actors who are willing to take anything thrown their way, that they sometimes don't know how to react when they encounter a working professional. I like to imagine that they sometimes stomp around their office cursing and pulling at their hair – right before they pick up the phone and book me.

MAKING WAVES

"I do not regret one professional enemy I have made. Any actor who doesn't dare to make an enemy should get out of the business."
- Bette Davis

When an actor asks for more money than the production company is willing to fork over, the usual line is, "We can't afford that – it's not in the budget." You're going to hear this over and over and over again. Much like a shopper saying, "I'm just looking" to a store clerk, you need to consider it as a standard response designed to make a problem go away. If you just shrug and say "ok", you are giving up too easily.

In most productions, actors account for about 3% of the total budget. That's not a lot. If they need to juggle their figures around to get the actor they want, they can usually make it happen. If they truly are on a razor thin budget and have no extra money to spare, then what are they doing trying to hire top level talent like you in the first place? Let them look around for some budget actor they can afford.

I swear, I have seen it happen a thousand times, but it still amazes me how quickly a "fixed" production budget can expand when it needs to. It's truly remarkable. Most actors never get a chance to experience this miracle for themselves, because they are afraid of "making waves".

Most actors are so convinced that their career hinges on being everybody's friend, that they're terrified by the thought of upsetting anyone. The truth is, when you stand up for yourself, it makes it easier for "business types" to identify you as a pro.

One of my first big jobs as an actor was for a relatively small production company. They were shooting a massive corporate video for a steel mill. It was an involved, film-style production and I was to play the lead. The non-union shoot was supposed to take place over seven days, and on the very first day we ran into massive overtime. I think I was on the set for about twelve hours, total. The same thing happened again on day two.

I began to get nervous. On a union production, talent is paid overtime after eight hours. On a disorganized shoot, this can quickly tally up to a small fortune. This was a non-union shoot, however, and I had a sneaking suspicion that they had no intention of paying me overtime.

I confronted the head-writer with my concerns (he was the man who got me the audition in the first place). He sympathized with me, but said "I'm sorry Roy, we haven't budgeted for overtime." To which I replied, "Well, that's a problem, because I expect to be paid for it." He shrugged apologetically. "Maybe next time we can make it happen for you, but for this shoot there's really nothing we can do. It's just not in the budget."

Now, I'm not the sort of person who goes looking for trouble. I have never enjoyed complaining or make a big deal out of things. But there are occasions in life when certain people will try to take advantage of you. When that happens, you are faced with the unwelcome choice of either standing up for yourself, or rolling over and being abused. I was not about to roll over. So this is what I did:

I told him I would continue to work on the shoot for the rest of the day, but that unless I had a document in my hand guaranteeing overtime pay, it would be my last day on the set. Furthermore, I made it clear that I expected overtime at the rate of "time and one half" for the first two hours over eight hours, "double time" for the next two hours after that, and "triple time" for anything beyond.

I can still recall the shocked look on his face. I meant every word, and he knew it. With a nod of stunned comprehension, he hurried off to "see what he could do."

While he was away, I informed the other actors of the situation. There were about ten of them sitting around in the green room. Disappointingly, not a single one of them stuck with me. They were all afraid to "make waves". They all agreed that we deserved to be paid overtime, but were convinced that if they made a fuss, the production company would never hire them again. I said I couldn't care less if they never hired me again, and everyone looked at me as though I was from Mars.

It wasn't long before my contact returned and discretely pulled me away from the others. He told me that the production was prepared to guarantee me everything I asked for, in writing. The document was being drawn up as we spoke. Their only request was that I "keep it under my hat and not mention anything to the other actors." Since I had already done that and been rejected, I agreed.

The result was that, on a shoot where most of the actors earned somewhere between two and three thousand dollars, I earned about fifteen thousand. We all did the same job. Most of the others were on the set just as long as I was and worked just as hard. But they had low day-rates and no overtime pay. But the story doesn't end there.

I assumed, along with all my fellow actors, that after raising such a huge fuss, my days of working with that particular production company were over. I couldn't have been more wrong.

To my surprise, they called me just two weeks later in order to book me again. That job was soon followed by another…and another…and another. In fact, this company was responsible for generating the majority of my income during my first year of acting. They were the reason I began to act full-time in the first place.

What is even more surprising is that in all the videos that I shot with this production company (there were well over a hundred) I never saw any of those other actors ever again. It was as if their careers came to a screeching halt. How's that for irony? They were so worried about "making waves" that they were willing to give up thousands of dollars in order to avoid it, and in the end, they got nothing in return. No work. No respect. Nothing.

There's a rather interesting post-script to this story: A few years ago I bumped into the assistant director of that nightmare production, now a successful director in his own right. In reminiscing about our old "war story", he happened to mention that the production company was paid 1.2 *million* dollars to put that video together. What's more, the entire project cost them less than $200,000 to produce – even with my "hefty" overtime. "Not a bad profit", he grinned. Nope. Not bad at all.

So much for, "It's not in the budget".

Don't go looking for trouble, but never be afraid of "making waves". Sometimes you have no choice. As long as you're justified in your position, you will not be considered a trouble maker. Indeed, you will more-than-likely be regarded as a true professional and treated accordingly. When you stand up for yourself, you earn respect. Allowing others to take advantage of you wins you nothing but contempt.

When problems arise on the set, don't even look at them as problems – look at them as opportunities, because that's exactly what they are; golden opportunities for you to prove to everyone that you are a pro.

EXTRA WORK

Everybody knows that extras are the bottom rung on the "acting ladder". It makes sense that when you're starting out in a business, there is going to be a period of time where you're going to have to put your dues in and learn the ropes. Most people naturally assume that means if they want to be an actor, they need to start out as an extra. This isn't the case.

Extra work has nothing to do with acting. Extras are bodies in the background. They may be walking down a street or sitting at tables in a restaurant behind the actors – but they are not actors themselves. Doing extra work is an effective way to show everyone in the industry that you are a starving, "wannabe" actor. Avoid it at all costs.

I give this advice to good actors all the time, only to see it fall on deaf ears. Actors consider extra work to be easy money. They like to kid themselves into thinking it's better than waiting tables, and at least they're involved with working in the industry. Who knows? They might even be "discovered" by somebody. Occasionally, it has been known to happen, but it's incredibly rare. In my opinion, it usually isn't worth the loss of credibility. There are only two times when I think an actor should consider doing extra work:

1. If you are asked to be an extra in a SAG commercial where the possibility of an upgrade exists. I think I've done this 7 or 8 times in my career, and I've been upgraded on three occasions. Those aren't bad odds. SAG extra work pays reasonably well (approx. $300 per day) and a lucky upgrade can net you many thousands of dollars.

2. If you are trying to make it as an actor in New York, it might be worth it to do some extra work on the soaps.

That's it. And even if you do that sort of extra work – keep it quiet. It isn't anything to be proud of. Do not put extra work on your resume.

If you are filling out a size card for a casting director in an audition and the card asks whether you would be willing to work as an extra – the answer is always, "no".

If you see a box in the casting director's office which says "place your headshots here if you're willing to be an extra" – don't even think about putting your headshot in that box. If your agent asks if you would like to be an extra – you don't. It isn't worth your time.

The response actors usually give me when they hear this advice goes like this: "But I can use the money, and it's not like I'm doing anything else." And these are the same people who complain when they're not included in the audition for a national commercial that pays $30,000 or more. Why should they be included? Those coveted audition slots are reserved for the top actors in town – not the bottom feeders.

Actors who do extra work are cutting their own throats. They are advertising the fact that they are starving actors. If you need the hundred bucks, then get a second job. You need to price yourself as an actor according to your value as an actor – not according to how much money you can make waiting tables.

It's tough to convince people that you won't act for less than $1500 a day, when you're willing to show up and sit around as an extra for $100 per day. That's a good way to ensure nobody (not even your own agent) takes you seriously. Let all the other actors shoot themselves in the foot. *Don't do extra work.*

TALENT AGENTS & YOU

There's a lot of information about talent agents available for free on the internet. There are also a number of books that have been written by agents, which provide valuable insight into their view of the industry. If you're new to acting, I encourage you to take the time to do some research in these areas. In this chapter, I'm going to stick to my theme of trying to provide you with something a little bit out of the ordinary: A working actor's perspective.

It might be possible to have a successful acting career without a talent agent, but I've never heard of anyone pulling it off. It certainly wouldn't be easy. Some regional actors try their best to circumvent talent agents (along with their fees) by working with corporations directly. I avoid doing this sort of thing because I believe it's terribly unfair to the agencies and rather short-sighted from a business perspective. There's nothing wrong with marketing yourself, but for various reasons that I will go into later, I think you would be wise to run all of your jobs through an agency.

There are good talent agents in nearly every region of the country, and finding them isn't as difficult as you might think. A quick search on the internet will reveal a list of agents in your area. Talking to local actors is perhaps the best way to find out which of these is the most reputable. You might also consider asking local casting directors for their opinions.

Keep in mind, legitimate talent agencies never advertise for talent. They don't have to, because they are already swarmed with actors.

Ads in the local paper for agencies *"Seeking new actors to play extras in upcoming feature films"* (or similar), are nothing but scams. Stay far away.

Legitimate agencies only make money when they book you on a job. Their percentage can vary from 10% to 20% – depending on the agency, their union affiliation, and the work. If you don't make money, they don't make money. A real agent may advise you to get new headshots, but the choice of photographer will always be up to you. Be wary of agents who insist on your using a specific headshot photographer. There's a good chance they are being paid a "kickback" to send you over.

After figuring out who the legitimate talent agencies are, the next thing most actors start to consider is how to go about approaching them. However, we're not like most actors. Therefore, the first question we are going to ask ourselves is, "Am I ready for an agent?"

Are you completely confident in your acting ability? Do you have great headshots, a resume, and have you received unsolicited, positive feedback from fellow actors or other industry professionals who have seen your work? If the answer to any of these questions is "no", then you're not ready.

Agents receive constant inquiries from people who are eager to break into the acting business. Most of these folks have no idea how the industry works, they're just calling for basic information. This puts a strain on an agent's time, which is normally pretty strained as it is. For that reason, cold-calling an agency flags you as an amateur, and dropping in on them in person is a definite no-no.

Unless you are already a well-established actor, by far the best way to land an agent is by having *them* come to *you*. Most actors lack the patience for that. They take a class, do one or two plays, and then assume they're ready for representation. Not so fast...

What's the point of signing with an agency – only to be lumped in alongside hundreds of other actors? That's the last thing you need. The whole idea is to stand out from the crowd. You want them to look upon you as a true professional from *day one*. If your focus is on signing with an agent, then you're going about it all wrong. You're behaving like a typical actor. Stop following the herd.

Forget about courting talent agents. Focus on improving yourself. When you perform in the classroom or on stage, don't strive to be adequate – strive to be excellent. Your goal is not to show people that you can act. Your goal is to blow people away with your acting. Accomplish that, and you will never have to worry about fighting for an agency's attention. They will be fighting for yours.

As long as you're operating outside the major markets, you will be working in a relatively tight-knit acting community. When people in this business spot talent, they are vocal about it. Just concentrate on doing good work, and let the rest take care of itself. Word will get around. If you're really good (and you had better be if you expect to make a living), it will spread like wildfire.

The only times I have ever approached agencies was when I first moved to New York and L.A. In both cases, I was already established and had no trouble finding representation. However, in every other instance in my career, the agencies have always come to me.

I can imagine what you must be thinking. "Ok, that all sounds great. But what if it doesn't happen? Suppose I take lots of classes and appear in local plays; I do good work and get positive feedback, but nobody refers me to any agencies? How long should I wait before submitting myself?"

That's up to you. Just because the people around you aren't telling you that you're brilliant – doesn't mean that you aren't. It's entirely possible that they don't recognize real talent when they see it. Of course, it's also possible that you don't have any real talent.

Then again, it could simply be a matter of your having a little more work to do before everything clicks into place. It's your career, and it's your call. Try to assess the situation objectively. You might try shaking things up by taking another class or performing with different actors. See if you can generate some fresh opinions. Rome wasn't built in a day. Chances are your empire won't be either.

I will say that if it means walking into an agency with your ducks in a row, holding all the cards – it's worth waiting a little while longer. Allow yourself the time to build self-confidence and develop your skills. You'll need them both in auditions. When you start doing really good work, people will be shocked if you're not represented. Everybody loves to think they've "discovered" a new talent. Let them spread your name around town and start the "buzz". Trust me, like bees to the honey – the agents will come.

THE AGENCY INTERVIEW

Let's assume that you've done good work in a class (or some other venue), and it has not gone unnoticed. You receive a telephone call from an agency that "so and so" has referred your name to them and said a lot of great things about you. They would like to meet you. You set up an interview. Now what?

You're going to treat this like any other professional job interview. You're going to show up fifteen minutes early, looking sharp. Have headshots and resumes ready to hand over for their review, as well as any DVD's or demo tapes of your past work, if applicable. Be sure to include your contact information on your headshots. You'd be amazed how often actors neglect to do this. Later, you will replace your numbers with the agency's contact info.

You should have a couple of monologues prepared, although you will rarely be asked to perform more than one. Avoid choosing a monologue with swear words and never perform something that causes you to yell or scream. You will be in an office environment and there will be people around you on the phone, so you want to keep things relatively low-key. They aren't remotely interested in how loud or foul-mouthed you can be. They just want to see how engaging you are, and whether or not you're believable.

Don't forget that a major part of this meeting is *you* interviewing *them*. Ask what sort of work they get. Is it mainly commercial, industrial, film, television, print, or all of the above? What sort of category or "type" do they see you as? It's also important to ask who else the agency represents in your category – and where they see you fitting into the mix. It's always a good idea to know who your competition is. You'll need to beat them in auditions if you expect to work on a regular basis.

Depending on how things go, the agent may offer to represent you either "freelance", or "under contract". This varies widely depending on the city you happen to be in. Personally, I think it's better to remain freelance when starting out, if possible, since it allows you the freedom to work with other agents and avoid putting all of your eggs in one basket. This also gives you time to see if you really "click" with one particular agency.

Lately, regional agencies seem to be more and more adamant about placing talent under contract. This isn't necessarily a bad thing, so long as you're getting regular auditions. It is a good idea to take the contract home before you agree to sign it though, just to look it over and understand its scope and limitations. Most contracts are for one year. Union contracts allow you to opt-out if you go 90 days without an audition.

Often, you might sign a contract for one aspect of the business and freelance for others. For example, it's common to sign an exclusive contract for film, television and commercials, but remain freelance for industrials. Ask around and talk to other actors to get a feel for what's considered to be "normal" in your area.

If you've followed my advice and the agent has contacted you, then you are in the driver's seat. There's no rush or obligation to sign anything right away. Tell them you want to meet with some of the other agents in town before you make a final decision. Then go out and contact those agencies. Explain who you are, and that you're considering signing with a competitor of theirs. You should have no difficulty getting an appointment.

FRANCHISED VS. NON-FRANCHISED AGENCIES

If you live in a "Right-to-Work" state, you will probably have a choice between franchised and non-franchised agencies. Right-to-work states do not require that you belong to a union in order to work. This is true of most of the southern states, as well as several in the Midwest. About half of all U.S. states are right-to-work.

Franchised agents are affiliated with the Screen Actors Guild (SAG) and the American Federation of Television and Radio Artists (AFTRA). They have to meet and follow a strict set of guidelines in order to be awarded franchise status.

Contrary to popular belief, you do not have to be a member of any union in order to sign with a franchised agency. This is true even in New York and Los Angeles. Being in the unions might make agencies more willing to talk to you, but you do not have to be a union member in order to be signed, or to audition. I'll go deeper into the pros and cons of union affiliation later. For now, let's stick with the talent agents.

Since franchised agencies are required to adhere to a strict set of guidelines (the most celebrated being that they are not supposed to charge their talent more than 10% commission), it is commonly believed that franchised agencies are better than non-franchised. While this perception is perfectly understandable, it is also entirely untrue. There are many non-franchised agencies throughout the country that do a superb job for their talent.

Sure, paying 10% commission is better than paying 15%. But what if the agent who charges 15% gets you 50% more work? What if they are really good negotiators, and can consistently book you for 20% over union scale? What if they consider you to be their #1 talent – and they go out of their way to get you into every possible audition?

Agency commission is just one factor that you need to consider. You will also want to take into account the agent's reputation around town, how many actors of your "type" they represent, how competent and organized they are, and how effectively you are able to communicate with them. Perhaps most importantly, you will need to assess how much they respect your ability. This can be difficult, because an agent's respect has to be earned, and it's on you to make it happen.

THE "A-LIST"

Every talent agency has their favorites. Often, these actors are referred to as being on the "A-list". Agencies take great pains to ensure these actors read for everything they are right for (and sometimes a good many things that they are not right for), because these actors have proven themselves to be solid bookers. Every actor wants to be on their agencies A-list, but surprisingly few know how to go about it. First, let's talk about what not to do.

Recently, a successful agent told me about an actor who really turned her off. Apparently, he approached her at a social function and asked, "What do I need to do to be on your A-list?" This question may sound harmless at first blush, and I'm sure the actor didn't mean anything sinister or sleazy by it, but it made the agent feel uncomfortable nevertheless. It's worth examining why.

The question insinuates that actors obtain their "A-list" positions via some form of favoritism. To a professional agent, that's insulting. It is more-or-less the same as asking, "How much butt-kissing am I going to have to do in order to be on your A-list?" Whether intentional or not – that's how it was perceived.

This fellow wasn't unusual in his reasoning; he was fairly typical.

Most actors seem to believe that the fastest way onto an agent's A-list is via "sucking up". They are mistaken.

Imagine a professional football player in his rookie year. He is eager to start for the team, but there are veterans in front of him who have already proven themselves time and time again. What can the rookie do? He decides to become best friends with his coach. He compliments him on his hair, bakes him an apple pie, and offers to wash his car. The coach is overwhelmed and immensely grateful. He introduces the lad to his prettiest daughter, and takes to calling him "son". Things are looking good…

And yet, when the season begins and the starting players are announced, the rookie is shocked to discover that he's a third-string bench-warmer. What went wrong?

No one can say he wasn't friendly, or that he didn't make an effort. But his effort was entirely misplaced, because it had nothing to do with *improving his game*. Professional football is highly competitive. You can be the nicest person in the world, but in the end, success or failure hinges upon your ability to perform, not bake.

It's exactly the same with acting.

There's nothing wrong with sending "thank you" cards and cookies. Agents work hard. When actors go out of their way to show their appreciation, it's always welcome. If you wish to show your gratitude in small ways – by all means, do it. Just make sure you're doing it for the right reasons.

Agents aren't stupid. They know when someone is kissing-up to them. If you seriously believe you're going to audition more often because you've brought them a tasty treat – you're only fooling yourself.

Forget about buying, baking, or somehow schmoozing your way onto an agency's A-list. It's never going to happen in a million years. There's only one way to get to the top, and by now it should be perfectly obvious. You're going to have to perform.

BRING THEM BUSINESS – NOT BROWNIES

"Things do come to those who wait, but only those things left over from those who hustle."

- Abraham Lincoln

You might be a fabulous actor, but unless you have a chance to show what you can do, the secret will die with you. Talent is useless without opportunity. Therefore, it is in your best interest to do whatever you can to create opportunities for yourself. There is nothing to stop you from marketing yourself to production companies and advertising agencies directly. It's a lot more work than just sitting around waiting for your agent to call, but actors who make the effort are usually well-rewarded. How can you make self-marketing work for you? Where do you even begin?

Start with the yellow pages. Every production company and ad agency in your area is listed. Pick up the phone and give them a call. Tell them you're a local actor and that you're curious as to whether they ever use actors in their productions. Some will say "no", others will say "all the time". Ask if it would be alright for you to come by their office and meet with them. If they are too busy, then see if you can at least send them your headshot and resume. They will almost always say "sure".

It's best to meet face to face if you can. That way you have a chance to actually make friends and (hopefully) charm them with your sparkling personality. A great many business people will be impressed by your assertiveness.

Remember, it's not as if you're an annoying door to door salesman. Unlike New York City and Los Angeles, actors in the regional markets are a novelty. Most people have never met an actor before. They're usually fascinated, and eager to hear about our careers. If you're in a local play – tell them about it. They might like to come and see it. They may even bring their families and friends along. Just one good contact can make all the difference to your career.

Even if you don't book jobs with any of the people you meet, you are still getting your name out there, and that's a good thing. These are industry people, and the sooner they know who you are, the better. Besides, one of the contacts you make might be good friends with somebody else who is looking for an actor. As long as you've been pleasant and friendly, your name may well be passed along. Soon, people you have never met or heard of will be calling you up and trying to book you for jobs.

I haven't marketed myself in years, but I still get these kinds of calls a lot. When they come in, I forward them to my agent and let her handle it. This is another area where I differ from nearly every other actor that I know of. Most actors who market themselves and generate their own business don't want to pay a commission to their agency and choose to work with the company directly. You can understand their point. After all, they went out and got the work themselves! Why should they pay a commission?

Actually, there are several excellent reasons.

First, the relationship between actors and agents is symbiotic. The success of one benefits the other. With that in mind, it's important that we look out for each other's interests. If companies could hire actors directly, how would the agencies survive? If your agent were to go out of business, how would that be good for your career?

Second, my goal is to build a business relationship with my agent based on trust and mutual respect. How is that possible if I am willing to go behind her back at every opportunity, just to avoid paying her a commission? If I were to do that, I'd be working *against* her. That's a great way to build resentment and hostility, but it's opposite of what I'm trying to accomplish.

Furthermore, agents exist for a reason. They play a vital part in any effective business negotiation. That's why all pro athletes use them. The problem with booking jobs directly and becoming too "chummy" with production people, is that sooner or later they are going to try to take advantage of you by asking for "freebies", or cut-rate pricing. Once you've become friends, it's impossible to say no without looking like a cheap-skate.

If you are a professional, you deserve to be properly paid for your services. It's always better to run the job through your agency. That way you get paid, the contact remains your friend, and the agency gets to play the role of "the bad guy". Good agents are prepared to accept that. They know it's their job.

There have been so many times when my agent has been able to obtain more money for me than I would have ever had the guts to ask for myself. In doing so, she has more than earned her commission time and time again.

Furthermore, when companies are slow to pay, I much prefer relying on my agent to hassle them for the funds, rather than being placed in the uncomfortable position of having to do it myself. Agents provide an important "buffer zone" between you and the client that you just can't get any other way.

Another reason to use your agent on all possible bookings is that it shows the world you're a pro. Everybody knows professional actors have talent agents. If a company calls you directly, politely give them your agent's number and inform them that your agent handles all of your scheduling. Anyone who is too cheap to pay your agent's fee is someone you don't want to work with in the first place.

Follow this advice and you will reap the rewards. While all the other actors are trying to get in their agent's good graces by kissing-up and trying to be their best friend – you will be handing them business. How's that for getting their attention? You want a sure-fire way to earn your agent's respect? You want to rocket straight to the top of their A-list? Bring them business – not brownies.

LET'S GET ORGANIZED

*"It is our responsibilities, not ourselves, that we should
take seriously."*

- Peter Ustinov

There are other things you can do in order to highlight your professionalism. Perhaps the most obvious is by ensuring that you are
organized. Agents love self-starters. Most actors are so completely
lacking in basic business and organizational skills that when an agent
finally comes across one who has their "ducks in a row" – it's like a
breath of fresh air.

It is worth taking the time to track your income through a software
program such as Quicken or QuickBooks. You're running a business
after all, and it's going to be important to know where you stand fi-
nancially. I keep track of all business affairs on my desktop PC. When
my agent calls for an audition or booking, I enter the information into
Google calendar. If you don't already know, you get Google calendar
for free when you sign up for a Gmail account. I find it to be handy,
because if I'm on the road and away from my PC, I can use my iPhone
or Ipad to enter and retrieve information. The updates sync between
my desktop PC, iPhone and Ipad automatically and instantaneously.
This makes things very convenient and allows me to have important
information at my fingertips regardless of which device I happen to
be using.

If you're watching your pennies at this stage and aren't ready to
fork over the cash for an Ipad or a laptop, a Day-Timer works just fine.
You can find one at any office supply store. Before I "went digital", I
used a three-ring Day Runner (size 8 ½" x 11"). This oversize version
has a sleeve inside large enough to store a manila folder full of head-

shots and contracts. You could use "Daily" or "Monthly" inserts, but I always found "Weekly" to be the most practical.

If you are going the Day Runner route, I also recommend picking up some blank note pages to keep track of the jobs you have done. Day Runner sells three ring "Things to Do" pages which work great for this purpose. When you complete a job, make a note of the date, client, and any important names or details – as well as the amount you are due. When your check comes in, just tick the small box on the right-hand side, indicating the job has been paid. In this way, you will be able to look back and see at a glance which checks remain outstanding.

Day Runners are great for actors because they're big enough to fit headshots inside. However, as we move further into the digital age, headshots and resumes are being sent via the internet more and more frequently. In the not-too-distant future, actors won't be carrying around physical copies of their headshots at all. As I type this, we're almost to that point now, but not quite. In any event, regardless of how you track your jobs and income, you need to know that it's important that you do it.

I always find it handy to take brief notes on every job that I do. I can't tell you how many times I've shown up at a job or audition and run into someone I've worked with before, who's name I can't remember. With my trusty notes at hand, I can quickly find what I need. I can also go back and see which jobs and roles I'm booking and which ones I'm missing out on. That helps me to figure out my strengths and weaknesses. Your notes could come in handy in a lot of other ways to, such as in a contract dispute, lawsuit, or tax audit.

Speaking of the tax-man, be sure to hang on to all of your acting-related receipts. As soon as you get rolling, consider meeting with an accountant to talk about what deductions you can and cannot take, as well as the benefits of forming a corporation for tax purposes. If a CPA is out of your price-range, there are several computer tax programs out there which are easy to use. I have always used Turbo Tax but there are many others to choose from. You can do your own research online, but don't trouble your agent with questions about all of this stuff. Financial advice isn't part of their job description.

While you are at the office supply store, you should also consider picking up something to keep track of your paystubs and contracts. An expanding, monthly file folder works great for this purpose. I pick a new one up each year, staple my paystubs to my contracts, and file them away as the checks come in.

That's really are there is to it! It doesn't take much to be organized; which makes it all the more inexcusable that so many actors aren't. Ironically, these are usually the same actors who get so frustrated when they have to repeatedly ask their agents to handle some mundane, organizational task on their behalf – and it doesn't get done.

I can understand how an actor might feel slighted when they need something taken care of (like the photocopying of a lost paystub, for example) and the agent doesn't get around to it for days, or weeks. I've been there myself. It's not uncommon for the actor to jump to the conclusion that their agent no longer considers them important, or at least no longer a priority. Resentment builds. Left unchecked, it can snowball and get out of hand. Before rushing to any hasty conclusions, however, it might be wise to step back and look at things from the agent's point of view.

A typical talent agency represents many hundreds of actors. If only fifty of those people call about a missing paystub, or some other minor piece of business which takes up no more than ten minutes of the agent's time, we're still talking about 500 minutes. That's eight solid hours of work, without any time for a lunch break. That is a full day that has to be set aside and devoted to solving minor issues; many of which were probably the actor's responsibility to begin with.

It's the actor's job to maintain their own records and finances. Every minute that an agent has to spend handling record-keeping on your behalf is a minute that they cannot devote to legitimate agency business. Dealing with the constant stream of actor requests, inquiries and minutia inhibits the normal work-flow of calls, submissions and bookings. It's an ineffective use of an agent's time and puts a strain on the entire operation. The result is that everyone's career suffers for it.

Unlike the overwhelming majority of actors, good agents are usually good business people. More often than not, they are also extremely busy. Besides the long work-day hours punctuated by constant interruptions, consider the extensive social obligations that litter an agent's calendar. Being a talent agent really is a full-time job, and agents have no choice but to prioritize their tasks. If you give your agent a low-priority issue to handle, don't be surprised if it is set aside to be addressed when time permits.

Low-priority tasks have a way of accumulating in a pile at the corner of an agent's desk. Unfortunately, the longer it takes to get to them, the more the pile grows. The bigger it gets, the more difficult it becomes to find time to deal with it. Before too long, a vicious cycle is born. In such a way, a relatively simple, five-minute task may go weeks without proper attention.

The actor who is unlucky enough to have an action item stuck within this pile needs to understand that they are not the one being regarded as "low priority" – their *task* is. So don't take it personally. Instead, do everything in your power to ensure that you don't contribute to that pile in the first place.

What can you do if you find yourself in this uncomfortable situation? Well, you might offer to come into the office and handle the matter yourself. If that turns out to be inconvenient for the agent, then you have little choice but to send occasional, gentle reminders, and remain patient. Remember, if the issue arose as a result of your lack of organization, then you have only yourself to blame.

AGENCY ETIQUETTE

Imagine having dinner at the home of a business acquaintance. You enjoy a nice meal, meet the family and perhaps play with the kids a little. Everything goes well. At the end of the evening, you shake hands at the door and thank your host for their kind hospitality. They tell you that you're more than welcome, and invite you to stop by and visit again anytime.

Taking them at their word, the next day you show up at their front door for dinner. The family is surprised to see you, but no less hospitable than the night before. They are so friendly, in fact, that you continue making surprise visits. How long do you think it would take to make a nuisance of yourself? A week? Two perhaps? I'm sure we can all agree that it wouldn't take long.

It's not much different with agencies. When you list with an agent, they will almost certainly tell you to stop by, keep in touch, or check-in from time to time and let them know what you're up to. They're not being disingenuous when they say these things, they really mean it. However, it's important to understand that they are also being polite. You would be amazed at how many actors don't get that.

Never go by your agency just to "touch base", "check-in", or "see what's up". If you walk through the door, you had better have a business-related reason for being there. The same applies to calling on the phone. Treat this as a hard and fast rule.

These days, most things can be discussed through email. Email comes with its own set of etiquette. Brevity is the soul of email. Keep your messages short and to the point. When an agent (or any business-person in a time-crunch) receives a massive "wall of text" email – it usually gets pushed aside for later. Sending long emails is an effective way to ensure that you will consistently be regarded as "low priority" – probably the last thing you're intending. Keep it short, use bullet points, then proofread it and take out all of the stuff that's "fluff" or irrelevant.

Suppose your email is running long because you have several matters to discuss? In that case, use separate emails – one for each topic. Since agents are organized, they tend to file their emails under subject headings. If you send your agent an email covering three different topics, how are they going to file it – or find it? These are normal procedures which everybody in the business world is aware of, but most actors are completely oblivious to.

In my experience, actors hate to communicate with their agents via email. It denies them the personal contact they so desperately crave. This need for agent attention is due to insecurity on the part of the actor – and every agent knows it. If you find yourself behaving in this emotionally needy fashion – stop! You're not doing yourself any favors, and you are in real danger of becoming a pain-in-the-neck.

I often hear from actors that they are afraid their agent is going to forget about them. If your agent is sending you on auditions – they haven't forgotten about you. If you are getting callbacks and/or booking jobs, I can assure you that you are foremost in their minds. Concentrate on doing good work and leave your agent alone. They're your agent – not your spouse. Let them do their job.

Sometimes you will have genuine issues that should be discussed in person. In those instances, it's usually best to call ahead and set an appointment. Following this advice might give you less "face time" with your agent, but your professionalism will not go unnoticed, or unappreciated. Every moment that an agent spends looking at your face in their office, is a moment that they can't spend looking at breakdowns and getting you work.

No Drama, Please

We are in the "drama" business, and Lord knows there is more than enough of it to go around. Unless your agent happens to be your real-life mom or therapist, don't treat them as if they were. It's perfectly fine to set up a time to talk about business related issues, but if personal problems have gotten you down – seek a more appropriate shoulder to cry on.

That's not to say you shouldn't communicate openly with your agent. On the contrary! I believe most problems that arise between actors and their agents can be traced back to a distinct lack of communication. I am always amazed by actors who seem to have no problem discussing personal issues with their agents, yet find it all but impossible to face them when they have a business related issue.

The fault lies with the actor, because it is the actor who desperately needs to be the agent's friend. Actors want to bond with their agents. So they have no trouble discussing personal issues, as well as their deepest insecurities. At the same time, when they have a problem with the way the agent has handled a business matter – these same actors are afraid to confront the agent, lest they create a rift.

Therefore, when actors have problems with their agents, they complain to other actors. That's not good, because it doesn't address the issue. These kinds of discussions usually amount to nothing more than "bitch and moan" sessions. Nothing can ever really be solved, because the agent is excluded from the discussion. All that usually happens is that the actor gets wound up tighter than a drum.

Then, out of the blue, the agent receives a note stating that (for whatever reason) the actor has decided to transfer to another agency. Not surprisingly, the agent usually comes away feeling stunned, amazed and quite possibly betrayed.

Suppose your agent sent you a letter one day saying that they were no longer going to represent you, due to your lack of performance – or for some other reason. Wouldn't you be shocked? You'd probably feel that you should have at least had a chance to present your case and discuss the issue before being shown the door – and you'd be right. Why can't actors give agencies the same consideration? No wonder everybody thinks we're flaky…

Agents are people too. They have their own needs, insecurities and personal lives outside of acting – just like you and me. Sometimes they make mistakes. Who doesn't? Bad mouthing your agency to other actors doesn't do anybody any good. If you have an issue with your agent, or are dissatisfied with their performance for some reason, set up an appointment and discuss it with them like an adult.

No matter how angry you may be, take care that you always go out of your way to keep things civil and professional. You might be surprised how, with a little honest dialogue, even major issues can melt away. If you do decide to part ways with your agency, you would be wise to do so in a manner that allows you to revisit again in the future. Don't burn bridges unless you have to.

INDUSTRIALS

"Remember: there are no small parts,
only small actors."

- Konstantine Stanislavski

Industrials aren't very sexy. There are no adoring fans or red car-pet premieres. When I first started out, like most young actors, I had no interest in doing industrials at all. Having worked for many dif-ferent companies, I had suffered through my share of tacky training videos. All of them seemed cheap and cheesy. I certainly didn't want to be associated with anything like that.

I have to admit though, it didn't take long for me to do a complete about-face. Today, I love industrials. If you are willing to open your mind and read on, I'll tell you why. Before I do that though, I suppose I should explain what industrials really are...

"Industrials" are usually corporate videos (they are almost never shot on film, although HD digital cameras are now commonly used). They cover a vast array of subjects, but as an actor, what you really need to be aware of is that your "role" within them will be classified under one of two categories: Either "Day player", or "Narrator".

The line between the two can sometimes get blurred, but a day player role usually means you are playing a character in a scene or series of scenes. More often than not, you will have a dialogue with someone else (though occasionally, it might be directly to the camera). The amount of dialogue can vary greatly and has no effect on the rate you are paid – unless you're able to negotiate more for the memorization required.

A narrator is the "host" of a video. As such, the narrator usually speaks directly to the camera and delivers the lion's share of the script. However, that doesn't mean they have more memorization and prep work than day players. Because of the volume and, on occasion, technical complexity of their lines, narrators often rely on ear prompters and TelePrompTers to make their lives easier. These devices require a certain amount of training and skill to use, which allows narrators to charge a premium for their services. Monetarily speaking, the difference between being a day player and a narrator is huge.

Currently, the SAG industrial day player rate is $471/day for Category I and $585/day for Category II ("Category I" simply means the video will only be shown "in-house" or, in other words, only to people who work within the corporation. "Category II" videos are intended to be viewed by end users, purchasers and/or the general public). Narrators earn almost twice as much as day players. The SAG rate for on-camera narrator/spokesperson is $857/day for Category I, and $1015/day for Category II.

It's important to understand that when we talk about SAG pay rates, we are talking about the *minimum* amount that an actor should be paid for these jobs. If you are good at what you do (and you had better be), you should be aiming to earn considerably more. How much more is going to depend on the market, and how good you are. I usually charge double SAG scale, but you might be able to charge more. As long as you are in demand, the sky's the limit.

Unlike student films or low-budget independents – corporations have plenty of money, and they are willing spend it. Most companies are aware of the bad reputation that training videos have, and they are eager to jazz them up in any way they can. That means spending more for higher production values and better talent.

All of this is terrific news for the actors who are willing to work in industrials. Surprisingly however, many actors are not. An actor once told me that he would never do industrials because he took his "art" seriously and didn't want to "sell out". To his mind, industrials weren't a legitimate means of acting, since they served no artistic purpose. Many actors seem to feel the same way. To me, that's utterly ridiculous.

In the first place, much of what takes place today on film and television can hardly be considered "artistic". In my personal opinion, 99% of the movies released in any given year have no artistic value whatsoever. They exist purely to generate income, and any artistic (or even entertainment) value is seen as a bonus. However, that doesn't stop actors from knocking themselves out to work on them.

So why all this irrational prejudice against industrials? I'll grant you they might not be artistic, or even particularly entertaining – but then again, they never claim to be. They exist purely to inform and educate. How is informing or educating people any less noble than entertaining them?

Not too many years ago, it was taboo for film actors to appear on television. TV was considered by most actors in Hollywood to be a "step down" from film. To a certain extent, it still is. But as the pay has improved, this stigma has become less and less prevalent. It seems that the right amount of money has a way of making the distasteful seem considerably more palatable to even the very best actors. This is also why an ever increasing number of movie stars are beginning to appear in commercials and voice overs.

There's nothing wrong with making money. It's a lot easier to function with it than without it. Working in industrials doesn't make you any less of an actor, and if you're exceptionally talented, there isn't any reason that I can think of why it should make you less of an artist, either. If you appear in an industrial film, no one will hold it against you if you happen be brilliant.

Okay, so besides the money, what else is great about industrials?

The experience! No matter how many acting classes you take, you cannot reproduce the knowledge and experience that you will gain from being in front of a camera on the set of a real production. The more you do it, the more comfortable you will be. The importance of this cannot be overstated. There are legions of actors who feel completely at home and confident up on a stage in front of hundreds of people. Put them on a set with a camera in their face, and they fall to pieces.

There's no way of knowing how well you will handle it until you do it. It's not that it's particularly difficult; it's just takes some getting used to. Like anything else, the more you experience life in front of the camera, the more comfortable you will be. You'll learn how to hit your mark, find your light, and work with sound and continuity. You'll learn how to stay consistent throughout takes. Most of all, you'll learn how to remain calm when all the focus, attention and pressure is on you to perform.

Is there really pressure on an industrial film? Of course! Just as there is with any other production in which real money is involved. This is why I say the experience can't be reproduced in a classroom atmosphere. Besides picking up a myriad of lessons necessary for acting in front of the camera, you'll learn an incalculable amount about the other aspects of production. What's more, you don't have to pay anyone for all of this experience and knowledge – they're going to pay you.

Industrials are nearly always shot using professional crew. Many of these people have been working in film and television production for years and are very good at what they do. Watch, listen and learn. Not only will you become a better actor, you might even set the stage for a future career as a director. Professional production people live and work in every region of the United States, as well as every country in the world. Regardless of where you happen to live, find them and make friends with as many of them as possible. They will lead you to where the work is.

This brings us to another positive aspect of corporate videos: Repeat business. Regardless of the region you're operating in, industrials will be a fairly niche market. Once you are "in" with the people who are producing them, you're in really good shape. I rarely audition for industrials anymore. The people who hire me know who I am and what I can do. Often, they will just call my agent, check my availability, and book me. From my perspective, it couldn't be easier.

Speaking of easy, if you are trying to get into the unions, industrials might be the path of least resistance. Videos shot under union contracts count toward unemployment insurance, health insurance and retirement just the same as if you were working in film or television. When it comes to pay and benefits, industrials are every bit as legitimate as those other media. There is no difference whatsoever.

As someone who is getting on in years, and perhaps becoming a little crotchety in my old age, I love the fact that it's possible to work on an industrial and still have a life. This is because the production hours are nearly always reasonable. While most films will expect you to be on the set by 6 am (I've been called in for makeup as early as 4 in the morning), and may keep you well into the evening – the typical corporate video starts around 9 am, and is wrapped by 5 o'clock. Often, it's much shorter than that.

Industrials also provide a certain amount of exposure for the actor. At this stage in my career, I've appeared in sales, marketing or training videos for hundreds of corporations. I also appear on a ton of corporate websites. All of this helps to get my image out in front of the public. Most people have probably seen me at one time or another. While this doesn't make me famous in any way, it does help to make me look "familiar" to many people.

The human mind has an amazing capacity to recognize faces. We may forget a name a few seconds after we hear it, but recognize a face instantly – even after not having seen it for years. I am often told that I look familiar, and I'm never quite sure if it's because they've actually seen me before, or because they're confusing me with someone else, but in the final analysis, it really doesn't matter. People tend to be drawn to what is familiar, therefore the more exposure you get as an actor, the more it helps.

Industrial films may also open up doors to other career paths you might never have considered. For ten years I found myself hosting an "Entertainment Tonight" type program for Continental Airlines, in conjunction with CNN. Being the host of a show is something that I had never remotely imagined myself doing. But, I wound-up making great money, and had a lot of fun doing it.

During the show's run, I had the chance to work with three female co-hosts who each went on to bigger and better things. Kathryn Carney became an anchor for CNN Headline News, Mia Butler hosts her own show, "Movie and a Makeover" on TBS, and Melissa Ponzio landed a recurring role on the hit television series "Army Wives".

So there you have it. Industrials may not sound all that glamorous to you, but don't sell them short. They're a terrific source of income and a superb way to learn the ropes and make valuable connections. What's more, there's no telling where they might lead.

TYPES AND USES

Until recently, training videos were probably the most common type of industrial video made. Every corporation uses them, and for good reason. Not only are they a tool for employees to learn about proper corporate policies, products and procedures, but they also provide the company with a certain amount of legal protection, effectively limiting their liability. In the litigious world that we live in today, training videos such as these are a must. There really is no limit to the amount of subjects and products that they might cover.

With the advent of high-speed internet connections and its common usage, more and more industrials are now being shot specifically for the web. Thus, an entirely new revenue stream has now been opened for actors. Companies are beginning to fall in love with the idea of having a spokesperson "step out" onto the screen when someone arrives at their website. When done well, it looks great.

Many of the larger corporations now have in-house production studios of their own. From there, they broadcast live shows to all of their stores regularly, as well as record videos to introduce new vendor products to their employees. In-house production seems to becoming more and more prevalent in businesses today. Companies have started to explore the idea of having their own "shows" which run on television screens in their lobbies. After all, if you have a captive audience sitting around waiting, why not saturate them with your products and services?

It's not just profitable businesses that are getting into the act, either. Many churches are now going "hi-tech" and creating their own production facilities. Some of the larger congregations broadcast on cable, or produce videos of their own. As the cost of high-quality cameras continues to drop, it's becoming more and more feasible for diverse groups and organizations to put projects together, which serves to create an ever growing need for actors.

Live presentations also fall under the "industrial" category. These are performed in front of a live audience, usually for business conventions or conferences. These jobs usually require the actor to be proficient in the use of an *ear prompter*. It's a long day on your feet, but the pay is excellent. Depending on the product, I typically charge around $1500 per day. Taking the time to learn how to use an ear prompter can really pay off for you.

EAR PROMPTERS

Ever notice the clear wire plugged into a news anchor's ear? It goes around the back of their neck, straps to the collar, and looks a little bit like a see-through telephone cord. That's an ear prompter. During news broadcasts, they are a discrete but effective way for producers to communicate with the anchor while on the air. Actors, presenters and hosts use them too, but in a completely different way.

Rather than connecting to another individual, an actor's ear prompter is plugged into a small, hand-held, digital recorder. The actor pre-records his lines into the device and upon the cue for "action", presses *play*. The actor then hears the lines of dialogue played into his ear, and speaks the words a second or two after he hears them.

As you might imagine, this isn't something most people can just pick up and do. It takes a lot of practice. However, if you're willing to make the effort, it's a skill that can set you apart from the pack and put a lot of cash in your pocket. Some actors make a very good living off of their ear prompter work alone.

It doesn't cost a lot of money to get started either. A small digital recorder can be purchased at Target, Radio Shack or any similar retail store for anywhere from $30 to $70, depending on the quality. The ear prompter equipment (wires, transmitter and an assortment of ear pieces) can be purchased from a company online called Audio Implements (www.audioimplements.com) for under $40.

You can always spend more, of course. There are wireless ear prompters available, but they cost around ten times as much and work about half as well. I used wireless prompters for about six years, but after switching to the wire version (as worn by newscasters), I have never gone back. I never will, either. The quality of sound is much better with the wired version, there is never any feedback from lights or transmitters, and since it comes with a wide variety of ear pieces, you can pick one that fits comfortably and snug – so there are no issues with the sound man hearing your prompter playback.

If you are a woman with at least shoulder-length hair, the wire will never be an issue. My hair is cut short (above my ears), so I have two prompters – a left and right-ear version. That way I can easily switch between them depending on how the shot is set up and which ear is closer to camera.

If you have an I-phone, mp3 player, or any similar recording device with headphones, you can practice your ear prompting without spending anything at all. Record a paragraph or two from a newspaper or magazine then play it back and try to speak the lines just after you hear them. It will be difficult at first, but stick with it and it does get easier.

Once you think you've gotten the hang of it, record a new speech and videotape your performance. Here are a few things to watch for and grade yourself on:

Are your hands moving in tandem?

They shouldn't be. It's ok to have them clasped naturally in front of you, but try to avoid chopping motions (very common) or motions in which one hand is behaving as a mirror image of the other. Move them independently, and naturally. Use them to help get the meaning of what you're saying across to the listener.

Are you blinking too much?

In normal speech, we blink when we register new information. People who first use ear prompters tend to blink far too much, because their mind is trying to register all of the information that's pouring into their ear. Avoid this, if possible.

Are your eyes glazed over?

It takes time to get used to, but the more you practice the more you will be able to relax and trust that the words are coming.

The hardest thing about using an ear prompter is making it look as though you're not listening to yourself – which creates that "glazed" expression. Your focus should be squarely on the camera lens, or whomever you're speaking to.

Does your voice sound normal?

You have to be able to speak naturally. Anyone watching should never be able to tell that your words are being prompted.

A lot of actors make the mistake of putting "proficient with ear prompter" on their resume, when they are far from it. Don't ever do that. There are nightmare stories of actors who claimed to be able to use an ear prompter, but found out the hard way that they couldn't. It's one thing to perform at home in front of a mirror, but quite another to do it with an unfamiliar (and possibly technical) script in front of complete strangers.

The first time you ever use an ear prompter on a real shoot, I would strongly advise you go out of your way to memorize as much of the script as you possibly can. In this way, you will literally be *prompting* lines that are already in your head. It will remove a ton of pressure from you when you get ready to perform. After you improve and become proficient, you won't need to bother with nearly as much prep time.

When recording your lines, start with a short countdown. I begin by saying "three…two…one…" and then I go directly into my lines. That way, when I press play, I have time to get my hand out of my pocket and get into position before I begin speaking. It also lets me know when my lines are coming up, so I'm not caught off guard.

Record small sections at a time. This makes it easier to keep things straight in your head. Don't record the whole script, or even large chunks in advance, because you never know what the director is going to want you to do as far as blocking (movement and action) is concerned. Wait until you receive your direction, *then* lay down the lines. Also, sometimes the script will go through numerous alterations on the set, which is another reason to record as you go.

Don't be afraid to communicate with the director and explain what you need. If the chunks of dialogue that they are trying to shoot are too long for you to handle, mention that it would be easier for you to take it in smaller bites. Most directors and producers have no idea how ear prompters work, and they are more than willing to make your life easier if they can.

TelePrompTers

TelePrompTers (yes, that is the correct spelling) are used extensively by hosts on industrial narration jobs – in addition to their traditional roles in television news, entertainment and talk shows. They are clever devices which allow on-screen hosts to read a scrolling script while looking directly into the camera lens.

The advantage of the TelePrompTer is also its downside, since the person speaking is *required* to look directly at the camera in order to retrieve their lines. This makes TelePrompTers tricky to use if the host has to look away for any reason – to talk to a guest, for example.

This limitation aside, TelePrompTers are far easier for most people to use than ear prompters. Unlike ear prompters, it doesn't take an inordinate amount of practice to attain proficiency. You just have to be a good reader. If you can pick up a script and cold read it naturally, you will probably be good with a TelePrompTer. Here are a few "tricks of the trade" for you to keep in mind:

You will notice two small arrows on either side of the prompter screen, about 2/3 of the way up. These mark the point where you should be reading your lines. The engineer will adjust the scrolling speed to suit your pace, so don't worry about the words moving too fast, or too slow. As with ear prompters, when using a TelePrompTer for the first time, you would be wise to become as familiar as possible with the script beforehand.

Sometimes you may see people on television reading a Tele-PrompTer and notice their eyes moving as they read. This is because the camera is too close to them. If the director tells you that he can see your eyes moving too much, ask him to back the camera further away from you. If he can't move the camera for some reason, ask the engineer to increase the font.

While actors who are new to ear prompters tend to blink too much, those new to TelePrompTers have the opposite problem; they do not blink enough. It's easy to get caught in a bug-eyed stare while reading, especially if you start to get tired. This happens a lot to novices because they aren't really thinking about what they're saying. Instead of simply reciting the words, you have to make a conscious effort to understand the meaning and implications of what you're saying. As your mind registers each thought, you will begin to blink properly and you will appear more relaxed and natural.

THE INDUSTRIAL AUDITION

All auditions are not equal, and you should not approach an industrial audition in the same way that you would a film or commercial audition. In preparing to read for an industrial, the first piece of information you need to know is whether you are reading for the part of a narrator, or day player. If it is a narration role, then you may use your ear prompter in the audition. If you do not yet feel confident enough to use your ear prompter in an audition, then you certainly aren't ready to use it on a job. Keep practicing.

Obviously, you need to know something about the company you are auditioning for. If you've never heard of them, do a quick search online and check out their website to bring yourself up to speed on the basics.

Many small to mid-sized corporations will post a biography of their CEO. Take a moment to read it. Oftentimes, (and nearly always in the case of small corporations) this is the person who will have the final say on who gets hired. Learning a little bit about this individual can be enough to provide you with a valuable edge. Information is power.

Some industrial auditions are held at the talent agency, some at the production company, and some at the corporation itself. When you show up, the first thing you need to do is sign in. If it is a union job and there is no sign in sheet, make a note of it and mention the fact to your agent afterwards. If you are kept waiting longer than one hour for a union audition, you are entitled to be paid for your time.

Your manner of dress will entirely depend upon the company you are auditioning for, and the role. If you're an employee, you want to dress as though you work there. If you're a spokesperson, you're going to more than likely be in corporate attire. It's really just common sense.

Some people wonder whether they should go "all out" for an industrial audition. For instance, when reading for the role of a doctor, should you show up in a lab coat? For industrials, it probably doesn't hurt to do something like that. However, don't go overboard and show up with lab coat, scrubs, mask, stethoscope and rubber gloves on. That's just ridiculous. It brings you back into the realm of looking like a desperate, starving actor again.

If the lab coat makes you feel more "authentic" and confident – go for it. If you feel silly and self-conscious, then don't wear it. Again, we are talking about industrial auditions only here. *Under no circumstances should you ever take a lab coat (or any other prop) into a film audition.*

Since the purpose of an industrial is to deliver information, the scripts tend to be somewhat verbose. Once the lawyers get hold of them and split hairs over every possible implication and subtext, what you are left with may sound very unnatural indeed. The temptation is to re-write your dialogue to make it sound conversational. Don't. They want to see whether or not you can say the lines as they are written. That's the "industrial challenge". Consider it an acting exercise. Do your best, and try to make it sound as natural as possible. If you're a good reader, you can take heart in the fact that most of the other actors are having an even harder time of it than you are.

One thing you can do to help matters is make contractions wherever possible. For example: If a line in a script were written, "I am happy to hear he will be there." You can say, "I'm happy to hear he'll be there." Contractions make the dialogue sound much more conversational, without changing the meaning in any way. This may seem incredibly simple and obvious, but when I sit in the lobby and hear other actors audition, I am often surprised by how few do it.

When you first receive your script, make sure you go over it thoroughly and underline the key words (such as the company name), as well as any facts, figures or product titles that seem important. Give these key words a little extra emphasis. Don't overdo it; just make sure they hear you pronounce them clearly. These marks will also make it easier for you to find your place on the page, should you happen to lose it.

While you are waiting to audition, there will probably be other actors hanging around. Auditioning in the regional markets can be very different from the majors, in that you tend to see the same people over and over again and it's easier to make friends. This spirit of friendly competition is great, because actors will often try to help each other out (in contrast to the major markets where they often try to psych each other out). Occasionally, however, these waiting rooms can become a little too social. Don't allow yourself to get caught up in that.

I am sure some actors think I am anti-social or even aloof because of the way I behave at auditions, but to be honest I don't worry about it. I'm not there to make friends, or catch up on what's been going on. I am there to compete for a job. It isn't my intention to ever be rude or unpleasant to anyone, but actors will occasionally try to talk your ear off, and there comes a time when you have to ask them to stop.

In this business, auditions are the whole ballgame. If you don't audition well, you don't work. It is as simple as that. Make sure your focus and attention is on the task at hand. When your name is called, you had better be buckled-up and ready to go.

There is no reason to be intimidated. You are not auditioning for the Queen. Hold your head up, look them straight in the eye and say "hello". Then find your mark and get ready to do your thing. When you are finished, say "goodbye" and leave. If more actors would do that, they would be better off.

Auditions are won while the camera is rolling. What you say before and after will never book you the job. It could, however, cost you the job. For that reason, I would advise against striking up irrelevant conversations or attempting to entertain everyone in the room with your sparkling humor. If they want to engage you in conversation – that's another matter. Just remember that it isn't the real reason you are there. Your chance to impress falls between "action" and "cut". Everything else is filler. Don't waste their time, or yours. Smile, be pleasant, then do your thing and leave. They will respect you for it.

THE INDUSTRIAL SHOOT

Once you have booked the job, the hard part is over. Now it is simply a matter of preparing like a pro, showing up on time and doing what you've been hired to do. If you are a day player, then you probably have some dialogue to memorize. I use my mini digital recorder to make this easier. Speak the lines of the other characters into the recorder, and leave blank space for your own. That way, you can play back the tape as often as necessary. Depending on how complicated your lines are, you should be able to memorize 10 or more pages of dialogue in about an hour. This little trick has been a life-saver for me on many occasions.

You'll probably be asked to bring several choices of wardrobe to the set. Make sure they're washed, ironed and neatly packed in a garment back. You might think this goes without saying, but you'd be surprised. I once saw an actor arrive on the set with his cloths wadded up into a ball, and jammed in a tiny duffel bag. It sounds incredible, I know, but some actors just don't have a clue.

The crew for an industrial is going to be basic. Besides the director you will have lights, camera, sound, and possibly a grip and/or gaffer. These folks are going to have their hands full, so stay out of their way and let them do their jobs. You're not expected to help or get involved with what they're doing in any way. Your responsibility is to know your script, and be ready to perform when asked.

Some actors (usually those who do a lot of stand-up comedy) seem to feel that because they are the "hired talent", it's their job to entertain everyone on the set. They do their best to keep everybody in stitches from the moment they arrive until the time they leave. This can be great fun at first, but there usually comes a point in the day when it starts to get really annoying.

Directors are nearly always in a pressure-packed race against the clock. The last thing they need is an actor slowing everything down for a stand-up comedy routine. Many actors crave attention. Like naughty classroom cut-ups, once they get a few laughs, and a little encouragement – they don't know when to quit.

This puts everyone on the set in the uncomfortable position of having to keep laughing, purely out of politeness. I have seen shoots slowed to a crawl more than once because an actor didn't know when to shut up. I'm sure afterwards they pat themselves on the back for having kept everyone in stitches all day. It must be all the more bewildering for them when they are never called back.

Remember why you are there. You have already gotten the job, so just relax. Focus on doing what you've been hired to do. If you do your job, everybody will be impressed.

Never say "Who wrote this thing?" when referring to the script – no matter how horrendous it might be. There is a good chance the writer will be standing in the room. Likewise, never make fun of the company or their products in any way – no matter how ridiculous it may be. It might seem trite or silly to you, but this is how these people make a living. It enables them to put food on their table and clothes on their children. You might think you are just lightening the mood, but there is a good chance your comments won't be appreciated in the least.

Be extremely careful about offering up suggestions to the director, producers or anyone else on the set, unless it is a matter that affects you or your character directly. Even if your suggestion is a good one, putting forward ideas as to how other people might do their jobs better makes you look ridiculous. This is true for all forms of acting – not just industrials.

Every crewmember's role on a set is clearly defined, especially on a union production. For instance, the soundman would never dream of moving the lighting man's cord without asking permission. Similarly, no lighting man would ever allow a soundman to move his cord; he would do it himself. Every job on a production has responsibilities and boundaries. Anyone who disrespects those boundaries is instantly flagged as an amateur. Actors are no exception.

As an actor on the set, your job is to be ready to perform when you are called, know your lines, and be willing to take direction. That is all. Actors who start giving the director suggestions on how to shoot a scene look like morons. Worse still, they risk pissing off the director by making him look incompetent in front of his own clients. As a general rule of thumb, it is good policy to mind your own business and refrain from making suggestions or giving advice unless you are specifically asked to do so.

Similarly, the script is your domain and acting is your area of expertise. You should never feel the need to apologize for blowing your lines or making a mistake. Every actor, even the greatest, screws up a line now and then. The difference between the professional and amateur actor is not whether or not they make mistakes, but how they handle those mistakes once they occur. Professional actors know that it is all part of the process and there is no reason to be sorry. Instead, they just hop back into position and get ready to try it again. Even if they have to do it 50 times, a pro stays cool and doesn't get flustered.

By contrast, amateurs allow themselves to get frustrated and bent out of shape. It reminds me of a mediocre tennis player who feels the need to smash his racket, stomp around and show off when playing badly. He's trying to send the message, "Sorry folks, I'm so much better than this", but message he really sends is, "I'm insecure as hell." It's embarrassing for everyone who has to watch it. If you find yourself becoming tense on a shoot – don't make a big fuss about it. Laugh it off. It will relieve the tension, help you to relax, and make everyone else on the set feel better too.

COMMERCIALS

While the goal of industrials is to inform and educate the viewer, there isn't enough time for that in a thirty second commercial. Instead, corporations try to elicit an emotional response. That's why so many commercials are funny (or, at least try to be funny). Laughter is probably the most commonly sought reaction, but it certainly isn't the only one. Commercials are designed to generate a range of human emotions, including fear, sympathy, envy, lust, nostalgia – even anger and frustration. Remember the advertisements for "Head on" pain reliever? Where the announcer kept repeating "Head On – apply directly to the forehead! Head On – apply directly to the forehead!" As much as those commercials made me want to hurl a brick through my television, I have never forgotten the name of their product.

Since ad agencies are going for emotional responses, they are searching for extremes. If they are trying to cast the role of a young mother, then they want someone who looks like she would be the perfect image of a young mother. If she is a cheerful employee, then she needs to be the ideal employee. If it is four slobs watching a football game, it's four of the biggest slobs imaginable. If the part calls for a middle-aged man talking about retirement plans, then he should come across as incredibly honest and trustworthy.

As an actor, you need to figure out where you fit into all this. Is there a niche that you can specialize in? What is your forte? Could you fill multiple roles? There is something out there for almost everyone. You don't have to be physically attractive to be a commercial actor.

You just have to know what your particular strength is, and then play to it as much as possible.

If you think you can play a young mother, then it doesn't make much sense for you to go out and get commercial headshots which make you look like a sexy seductress. Your hair, makeup and clothes should all be in line with the general public's image of the ideal mom. If you are an elderly gentleman who might be able to play the sincere, honest roles often required by banks, medical companies and so forth – then don't go out and get commercial headshots where you have a big, beaming smile that makes you look like a politician or a used car salesman.

Take a close look at the commercials you see on television and start to form some ideas about where you may fit in. In which commercials would you cast yourself? Observe these closely and let them be your guide. How do the actors dress and behave? You may need to buy yourself new clothes or change your hairstyle in order to fine-tune the image you are going after. Keep all of the receipts to write off on your tax return later.

When it comes to clothes for commercials, there are some rules to keep in mind. Stay away from anything that has a busy pattern. Solid colors are usually best. Avoid wearing black or white, as well as anything with a logo (such as the Izod alligator). Layers are commonly used in commercials. They just look better on camera. Everything must be neat clean, and ironed – even if you're reading for the role of a "beer drinking slob". Wrinkles don't exist in commercials.

Many of the tips and tricks of the trade that I went over for industrials apply to commercials as well. If you are handed 30 seconds of copy when you show up at the audition and do not have time to memorize your lines – concentrate on memorizing the *first line*. Once you have gotten that down, then memorize the *last line*. These are by far the most important parts and you want to be sure that you nail them both.

The "star" of the commercial is the product that is being sold. In advertising, that's why it is often referred to as, "The Hero". As with industrials, you should understand that this product is what puts food on the table for the people who will be deciding whether or not you are going to be in their commercial. Therefore, take care that you treat and refer to it with the utmost respect – no matter how silly or ridiculous it might be.

One more thing: Never write yourself off. The first national commercial that I booked was for Ford Motor Corp. They were looking for a man in his early 40's to play the role of a father with a teenage son. Since I was only 26 at the time, I assumed I had no chance. The only reason I went to the audition at all was because I had been begging my agent to use me as a "ringer" for some time (A "ringer" is an actor who doesn't fit the specifications the ad agency is looking for, but whom the agent submits nonetheless). Now that my agency was using me as a ringer, I couldn't very well turn the opportunity down.

To my surprise, I booked the job! The ad agency liked me so much that they re-wrote their script and gave me a four-year old son instead. You just never know.

THE COMMERCIAL SHOOT

When you show up on the set of your first commercial, you will immediately notice that there's a lot of action going on. Commercials (especially union commercials) are much bigger productions than industrials. Besides the larger crew, there will often be multiple representatives from the corporation and ad agency in attendance.

Soon after you arrive, you may be asked to sign a "talent release form". This is your first opportunity to show them how much of a professional you are, because unless your agent has already seen this release ahead of time and given you the "ok" on it – you are not going to sign it.

There's no need to be bitchy about it. Just shrug and tell them you can't sign a release until your agent has looked it over first. If they tell you that your agent *has* already looked it over, just say they never mentioned anything about it to you, and that you need verify it with them before signing. Don't worry about hurting anyone's feelings or "making waves" here. This is business. It is also your neck on the line. The last thing you want to do is sign a document giving away your rights for little or no compensation.

Production companies should know better than to do this, but it happens all the time. More often than not, they either forget to go through the right channels or just don't take the time to do it properly. It is usually an honest mistake. However, in some cases they really are trying to be sneaky and "pull one over on you"; better to be safe than sorry.

There is a chance that they might try to intimidate you and make a fuss over this. They may even go so far as to threaten not to use you in the commercial at all. That's fine. You have already been booked and they are going to have to pay you no matter what. In the end, when they realize you are not only in the right – but hold all the cards, they will calm down. Usually, it ends up not being such a big deal after all.

Most actors dread this sort of confrontation, but to be honest, I rather enjoy it. It gets my blood pumping. I look at these situations as a chance to show my mettle and prove that I'm not some wishy-washy newbie that can be easily intimidated. When this situation arises (and it will if you do a lot of commercials), look upon it as a golden opportunity to show them that you're a pro.

Commercial acting has a style and technique all its own. The popular image of the typical commercial actor is of someone with a big, toothy smile who seems fake and over-the-top. While this may often be the end result, it is almost never the intended result.

Over-acting in commercials usually happens as a result of a tug-of-war that takes place between the director and the actor; which the director ends up winning.

Since commercials deal in extremes, the director will often do his best to push the actor to behave in extreme ways. For instance, if you're eating a bowl of cereal – you're not just enjoying it, *you're blown away by how fabulous it tastes*! Meanwhile, actors know the performance has to be realistic – so they try to pull back to avoid over-acting. Thus, we have the tug-of-war; the director always trying to get the actor to do more, the actor always trying to do less. When you see over-the-top-acting in commercials, it doesn't necessarily mean the talent couldn't act. Usually, it was the director (or client) who pushed them to that extreme.

On big-budget commercials (with better directors), this isn't such a problem. Good directors understand that there is no point in trading realism for false-enthusiasm. Likewise, top ad agencies are smart enough to know that the extremes they are after are more effective when they arise from outrageous situations, rather than over-the-top acting.

Regardless of the subject matter, actors are only truly convincing when they are sincere. The next time you're directed to "smile bigger" or "be happier", make sure that you never lose a sense of sincerity in what you're doing. Always try to keep it real. The final result will be better for it.

Even though the movies are considered to be a "higher" form of acting, working on a commercial can often be more difficult than performing in a feature film. In a movie, for the most part, the lines are yours to deliver as you see fit. If it seems more natural for you to say them in a slightly different way, you are nearly always allowed to change the words. Sometimes you're given a tremendous amount of leeway. Not so with commercials.

If you have lines to speak in a commercial, you can be sure that *every syllable* will be scrutinized by the clients and advertising executives. You may be told to give one word slightly more emphasis and another one less. The use of specific words and phrases may be debated, adjusted and altered as necessary. You will often be given awkward "sales pitch" terminology to say, and expected to deliver it conversationally. You must be word-perfect. You will also be expected to deliver your lines within a set time-frame.

For example, in a 30 second commercial, you might need to deliver your lines in 28 seconds in order to leave room for the tag. Not 27 seconds, not 29 seconds – *28 seconds*. This is easier to do than it sounds, so don't worry about it – you'll soon get the hang of it.

In between shots, one person might be fussing with your hair while another one pats makeup and powder all over your face. It's hot under those lights, so powder has to be reapplied often in order to keep you from glistening with sweat. While this is going on, you should be focusing on how to deliver your lines properly, and in the allotted time frame, while remembering any other instructions you may have been given.

After several frustrating attempts, you may finally deliver your lines perfectly – only to have a plane fly overhead in the middle of your performance, ruining the sound. The next take might get blown due to the boom man dropping his microphone into the shot, and on the next try – maybe the cameraman misses his focus. Mishaps such as these (and thousands of others) are all part of the process. As a professional actor, you are expected to stay cool and handle all of it with patience, grace and good humor.

COMMERCIAL PAY

I am often asked how much commercials pay. The truth is that there is no easy way to answer that question. It's extremely complicated and there are a great many factors involved. SAG commercial pay for principal performers depends upon the amount of viewers located within the regions where it airs. It also depends upon how long the spot runs. Figuring out exactly how much you're going to make for any union commercial can be difficult, but you can find the latest figures for SAG rates online at http://www.sag.org/content/commercial-contracts.

It's possible to make a lot of money on a commercial, but regional commercials typically pay somewhere between $2000 and $10,000. The total amount that you will make depends upon a myriad of factors, including the length of run and the regions in which the commercial airs. If you have a spot that airs in the larger television markets, you can make much more.

For non-union commercials, it all comes down to negotiation. Most non-union cable spots will try to get away with paying $500 for the shoot and anything from $500 to $1000 for a year of usage. Whether or not you think that's sufficient is between you and your agent.

When negotiating rates, you need to keep in mind whether or not the commercial will create a conflict for you. A conflict is where you are taken out of a particular commercial segment, because you are already representing a company in that segment.

For example: If you do a commercial for Burger King, you are going to have a conflict for fast food restaurants. You will not be able to audition for any other fast food organizations in the same market while your Burger King commercial runs. Violating this is a good way to get sued.

If you are fortunate enough to achieve even minor celebrity status, the amount of money that you can command for a commercial can go up significantly. I personally know of one instance where the host of popular cable television program was hired to do a series of 30 second commercials for a car company, and paid $250,000 for each individual spot. Not too shabby. It's enough to make me seriously consider becoming a cable TV host.

FILM & TELEVISION

"I am proud to have been in a business that gives pleasure, creates beauty, and awakens our conscience, arouses compassion, and perhaps most importantly, gives millions a respite from our so violent world."
- Audrey Hepburn

"I felt like an impostor, taking all that money for reciting ten or twelve lines of nonsense a day."
- Errol Flynn

I don't think it's a stretch to say that most actors dream they will eventually enjoy some level of success on the big screen. Leaving the matter of fame aside for now, working regularly in film and TV gives an actor credibility that no amount of training can provide. Perhaps it's because these roles have to be earned the hard way. In order to land a day player role in a major film, an actor may have to beat out scores (possibly even hundreds) of competitors. Is it worth the effort? You bet it is! Not only for the boost of legitimacy that it gives to your career, but for the cold, hard cash. When everything lines up just right, the money for even a minor role can be staggering.

The first feature film that I was cast in was "The Patriot", starring Mel Gibson. I had a minor role as one of the redcoats that burned his house down. I had only one line: "Rebel dispatches, sir." Not exactly Hamlet.

Even so, I still had to audition for the part. And after the first audition, I had to survive two more callbacks before landing the role. That might sound like a lot of trouble for a character with one line. Some may even wonder if such a small part is really all that much different from being an extra. Take it from me…it is.

At the time "The Patriot" was made, SAG union extras were supposed to be paid about $90 a day. However, since everybody wanted to be in a Mel Gibson movie, and we were filming in non-union North Carolina, many of the extras were working for $15 a day. Some of those days wound up being 12-14 hours long. Everyone was dressed in wool overcoats and loaded down with army gear, so we were hot. Not surprisingly, new extras had to be constantly recruited to play the redcoats, because there were desertions all the time.

It sucks to be an extra. On every movie set, craft services will set up a table full of snacks, fruit, sandwiches and drinks for everyone to munch on. Everyone except extras, that is. Extras aren't supposed to go near it. When lunch and dinner are served – extras are the last to eat. Extras are expected to stay out of everybody's way and keep to themselves. They are not supposed to eat, sit or speak with the cast – indeed, on some film sets extras are specifically instructed to avoid even making eye-contact with them!

I remember during one particularly hot afternoon on "The Patriot" when the extras were forced to stay out in the sun in-between setups, while all the available shade was reserved for the cast. In my opinion, being a movie extra is a bit like volunteering to become sub-human.

By stark contrast, during my two weeks of filming, I was treated like a prince. I was lodged in the same hotel as Heath Ledger and paid a generous per diem. While on the set, I had my own room in an air-conditioned trailer. It was small, but large enough to relax and grab a nap between shots. On the set, I mingled with the stars. It made no difference that my role was miniscule. I was considered to be one of the "artists" by both cast and crew. When the movie opened in Los Angeles I was invited to attend the red carpet premiere along with the rest of the cast.

With overtime, I was paid around $5000 for my work and I received that check within thirty days. When the film was released to the theaters – I got a check for that same amount again. I received the same amount again when the film was released to the overseas markets, and yet again when it went to DVD.

It didn't stop there. I got another check when the film went to television and even now – thirteen years later, I still get residuals in the mail on a semi-regular basis. There's no telling when they are coming or how big they will be. Sometimes they are only a few dollars, sometimes they're a few hundred. Still, not bad for three words, eh?

With one line of dialogue, it might seem strange that I would be on the set for two weeks, but that's how it is in the movies. There were a lot of complicated scenes to shoot – many of which I had no part in at all. We also shot some scenes that were cut from the final version of the film, and there were several days when we couldn't shoot anything because of the weather. It all adds up.

You might think I hit a home run with my first film role. Far from it. A home run would be more like what my friend Lenny hit when he landed his first role in a movie. The film was *"Forest Gump"*.

Lenny played the "Young man running", and he had only two scenes. When Forrest Gump decides he is going to run across America, Lenny is the guy who comes up to him and says, "You're Forrest Gump? You're my hero! Can I run with you?" Later in the film, when Forrest decides to quit running in the desert out west, Lenny says, "What are we supposed to do now?"

That's it. Doesn't sound like much, does it? But Lenny was credited with three months on "Forrest Gump", even though he only actually worked a few days. It turned out that way because the first scene was shot on the east coast, and the second scene couldn't be shot until the production moved out west. Lenny was held over, and paid for all the time in-between. While he was waiting to shoot his second scene, Lenny got to hang out at home. His only directive? Grow a beard.

With my three-word scene in the Patriot, I made enough to buy myself a car. Lenny made enough to buy himself a house. As a matter of fact, he did buy a house. Soon after completing "Gump", he made the move out to L.A. and plunked down the cash for a beautiful new home. I'm sure he still gets healthy residual checks, even today.

So the difference between an "extra" and a "day player" is monumental. If you land the right part in a decent film, you can make a small fortune playing even a minor role. There's a lot of money in the movies. Remember that when you start to negotiate your rates.

PREPARING FOR THE AUDITION

"You can't wait for inspiration. You have to go after it with a club."
- Jack London

Most casting directors in the regional markets will accept headshot submissions directly. However, in order to be taken seriously, it looks much better if you are submitted via a talent agency rather than doing it yourself. Casting directors are the gatekeepers to film and television, so it's important to make a good impression on them. Despite their title, a casting director rarely (if ever) has the final word on who gets the part. Their real job is to separate the wheat from the chaff, and decide who should be seen in the first place.

Let's assume you have an agent, and that he or she has set up an audition for you with a casting director for an upcoming film. What do you do now?

Well, if you only have one line like, "Rebel dispatches, sir" – there isn't going to be a whole lot of preparation necessary. You're just going to walk into the room, hit your mark, and imagine yourself in the scenario as best you can. Then you're going to say your line in the most believable way possible. In these instances, you are going to be cast based on whether you look and sound convincing in the role.

These "one liner" parts are probably going to be the way you start out. If the casting director likes what you do, they may ask you to read for something bigger. Occasionally, you will be handed a new script and given a few minutes to look over it in the waiting room. In "cold read" situations such as this, you're not expected to know the lines perfectly, so don't worry about that – just be familiar with them. As a matter of fact, you should never worry about being word-perfect. No one cares about that in a film audition. Instead, focus on communicating and listening. Keep the script in your hand, but don't refer to it unless you absolutely have to.

If you're given a larger role, with adequate time to prepare, then you are going to have homework to do. Strolling into the casting office without doing your homework is going to flag you as an amateur.

What does homework entail? For most actors, it is simply a matter of memorizing their lines. As is so often the case, you should take care not to follow their lead.

The first thing you need to do is read the script you've been given in its entirety. Read *everything*. This includes the stage directions and the parts that have been crossed out and do not apply to your scene. The more you know about the project, the better off you will be. Lots of actors completely ignore the stage directions because that's what they've been told to do in acting class. Ignorance may be bliss, but knowledge is power.

Stage directions are there for a reason. They provide valuable information. When I auditioned for the role of *Bob Gardner* in *"Bobby Jones: Stroke of Genius"*, Rowdy Herrington told me I was the first actor he'd seen all day who had read the stage directions and understood the scene. Pretty shocking. For all I know, it could have been one of the main reasons he cast me in the film.

Once you've read the stage directions, you can always choose not to follow them. It's up to you. However, at least you will be making an informed decision, rather than an ignorant one.

As soon as you've read everything and you understand what's going on, go back and read through the script again. This time, for each of your lines, ask yourself the question: "Why am I saying this?" *Make sure you come up with a clear and specific answer for each and every line of dialogue.* The more specific your answer, the better.

After you've answered "why" for each line of dialogue, go back and read the script again. This time, focus on who you are talking to. Who is this person to whom you are speaking? What is your relationship with them? If you decide that you don't have a relationship because you've just met them – that's a bad choice. It's boring. Surely you must have an opinion? What is it?

Have you ever met someone in real life whom you instantly detested – or immediately found yourself attracted to? Why couldn't you feel that way about the person in this scene? Either choice is better than apathy.

Stretch yourself. You could choose to be the perfect housewife, but isn't it more fun to be someone having a sordid affair on the side? Or with some other secret to hide? Characters with faults are so much more compelling.

Once you know who you are talking to, what your relationship is and how you feel about them, you need to figure out what it is that you want in this scene. What are you hoping to achieve with your dialogue? You must want something, or you wouldn't be speaking. If your goal isn't obvious, then pick something to fight for. It can be love, revenge, lust, or perhaps something else entirely. The more important it is to you, the more compelling you will be.

When you have figured out what you want, go back and read the script *again*. This time pick at least one point where you are going to change. The change can be physical, intellectual, emotional – or any combination of the three. This is going to be your transition. Transitions need to happen in every audition. It's where we see you change as a result of something that has happened in the scene. This change can take place at the beginning, middle or end. There can sometimes be more than one transition, but there must always be at least one.

Here again, if you don't see an obvious transition written into the scene, then create one. This is a tremendous opportunity for you to bring something to the table that nobody else has envisioned. Don't worry about doing it "wrong". There is no wrong! That's the fun thing about auditions. Later, when you are cast in the role, there will be plenty people giving you input and telling you what you can and can't do. The audition is your time. It might be the only time that the role is completely yours, and your one chance to play the part exactly the way you think it should be played. Don't let that opportunity pass you by.

Once you have done your homework by answering these questions, you will be amazed how well you know your lines, even though you've put zero effort into memorizing them. That's because once you have the essential questions behind what you are saying, the words will come to you naturally. The last thing you want to focus on in a film audition is your lines. Your focus should be on listening to the other person, and communicating your message. This is called "being in the moment".

When you are truly "in the moment", you have no idea what is going to happen next. You are not sure what the other person is going to say until the words come out of their mouth. You have to listen, process what you hear, and respond to the new information. It's fine if you have to struggle a little over your choice of words. We do that in real life all the time.

Again, don't worry about getting hung up on specific words in a film audition. No one is going to be upset if you aren't word-perfect. It's infinitely more important that you understand the meanings and intentions behind the words. If you are communicating, listening and reacting naturally, no one cares if you blow a line. They probably won't even notice.

Practicing your audition in front of a mirror is a really bad idea. All that does is help you to start "posing" and focusing all of your attention on how you look. As an actor, that's the last thing you want.

Pick a point on a wall, a photograph, or better yet, an actual human being – and focus on communicating your message to them. If you want to critique your audition, then record yourself on camera, or have a friend do it for you so that you can go back and look at your performance afterwards. Again, the great danger here is that you will become overly self-conscious about your appearance.

Once you feel that you are fully prepared – it's time to throw away all preparations. Go through the scene again in an entirely different way. You might forget your lines when you first try to do this. That's because you've begun to associate them with specific choices and feelings. Shake everything up by saying all of your lines as though you're angry – then say them all again as though you're happy. Try other emotions. You'll be surprised how often you discover interesting choices and transitions that would never have occurred to you otherwise.

It might be tempting to skip this last part of your homework, but don't. When you audition for a director, there is always a chance that he or she will ask you to do it again in an entirely different way. This is how you prepare for that possibility, just in case.

Do your homework properly, and you will never have to worry about forgetting your lines. Once you are relieved of that anxiety, you can let go, fully engage your imagination, and lose yourself in the moment.

THE AUDITION

When you arrive at the audition, the first thing you need to do is sign-in. If it's a union shoot, there will be a space where you are supposed to write your social security number. Don't. It's too dangerous to have your social security number out there for everybody to see. Just write "on file" instead.

The first thing a casting director will often do is ask whether or not you have any questions. The correct answer is "no". Some actors panic, and feel the need to come up with a question on the spot. This is not the time to ask about characters or anything else related to the script. Making all those decisions was part of your homework. If you didn't do it, it's too late now.

The only legitimate questions you can ask are with regards to the audition itself – not the script. For example, if you are supposed to react to a noise, you might ask whether someone is going to make a noise for you to react to, or if you should just imagine it. Some actors ask how tightly they are framed. That's a legitimate question in a commercial or industrial audition, but not in film and TV. You should always assume that you are framed tight (head and shoulders), and play the scene that way – unless specifically told otherwise.

Never mime anything in an audition. If you are supposed to be talking on the telephone, don't hold up an imaginary phone to your ear – use your cell phone instead (make sure it's turned off). If you are supposed to flash a badge – flash your driver's license. If you are supposed to shake hands with someone – don't pretend to shake hands with an imaginary human being; wave instead, or smile.

Never bring props to a film or television audition. You can get away with it in industrials and perhaps low-budget commercials, but not here. Not ever. Using props exposes you as a rank amateur. For our purposes, a prop is anything that at least 50% of the population outside doesn't normally carry on their person every day.

For instance, everybody has a cell phone, so a cell phone is not a prop. It's fine to use one in an audition (but again, make sure it's turned off!). A water bottle is not a prop. Tons of people carry water bottles around with them all the time. If you are supposed to be drinking coffee or a beer in your scene – drink from your water bottle, instead. Props are things like fake guns, lab coats, uniforms, cowboy hats (unless you live out west, where they are commonly worn), binoculars, stethoscopes and so on.

You can look the part, without showing up in a costume. For instance, if I'm reading for a doctor, I'm not going to show up wearing scrubs and a lab coat. Instead, I might wear a button down shirt and some khakis. Usually, I'll try to imagine how the character would look after work, or on the weekend.

Hold on to your script throughout the audition. Since you are expected to have it with you, a script doesn't count as a prop! It is perfectly acceptable for you to use your script for whatever you need it to be: Legal briefs, a golf club, an envelope full of money, a rifle – whatever.

Some actors wonder how this is different from miming. After all, is using your script as a gun any different from holding up an imaginary phone to your ear? You bet it is! Your script is *tangible*. It doesn't weigh much, and it may not look remotely like the object you're using it for, but it is infinitely better than miming with thin air. Miming just looks silly in a film audition.

Ok, but surely it must be fine for you to bring a prop to an audition once in a while, right? I mean, what if you're supposed to be a golfer, and you've got golf clubs in the back of your car, why not bring a club into the audition? Is it really such a big deal?

Yes, it is a big deal – and you should never do it. Bringing a prop into an audition makes you look hungry. Remember the cardinal rule? *Nobody hires a starving actor.* In a film audition, you have to play a little Takeaway. Walk in the room as though it isn't the most important thing on your calendar for that day, and use whatever is available to you at the time. To go along with this, there is an old saying among veteran actors that you should never buy anything specifically for an audition, including clothes. Doing so ensures that you will not be cast. I'm not saying this is a hard and fast law, but it is a good rule of thumb. In any event – no props!

Back to your audition: Keep the script in your hand. If you put it down, you are indicating to everyone watching that you are giving a finalized performance. That's not the impression you want to give them, because they are liable to assume this is as good as your acting will ever get. With the script in hand, you reinforce the fact that you have only had a limited amount of time to prepare, and on the set you would be even better. Also, should the wheels come off in the audition and you find that you are completely lost, you don't have to fumble around for the script – you've got it right in your hand.

You will be asked to stand on your mark (usually indicated by a piece of tape on the floor) and "slate" your name, as well as the role you are reading for. Do not turn this into a mini-monologue. Just state your name, and the name of the role. That's it. This is not the time to greet and charm everybody – just give them what they ask for.

Incidentally, in L.A. it is now considered somewhat politically incorrect to say that you are "reading" for a part. Anybody can read; actors act. Even though Hollywood isn't the beginning or end of filmmaking, it still sets the standards for what is cool and acceptable in the audition world, so we should follow their lead in this respect.

With that in mind, I would slate for the role of "Deputy Bob" like this: "Roy McCrerey, and I'm Deputy Bob". Or even, "Roy McCrerey; Deputy Bob". Keep it that simple and straightforward. Don't be like some actors and say, "Hello, how are you this wonderful day? My name is _____, and today I'm going to be performing in the role of Deputy Bob for you!" Slating like that is the audition-equivalent of shooting yourself in the face.

Never look into the camera lens during a film audition (other than the slate). The same is true for television, unless you are auditioning for the role of a host. Look directly into the eyes of the person who is reading with you. Listen to them and communicate with them. *Stay in the moment.*

WHAT THEY WANT TO SEE

It goes without saying that directors will expect you to be able to deliver the lines naturally, and in your own voice. They are not looking for someone who can *play* a particular type; they want someone who *is* a particular type. This is why you should walk into the room convinced in your own mind that you are the character in question.

As incredible as it might sound, the camera can record your thoughts. Not in specifics perhaps, but it will show whether or not you believe what you're saying and doing. It's also obvious when you are focused on yourself. Focus on communicating and forget about everything else. To communicate effectively, you're going to have to listen.

Listening is one of the most important criteria that directors will look for in an actor. Think about having a conversation with someone you love. You can tell in an instant when they aren't listening, can't you? Even if they're looking directly into your eyes, you can see when their expression glazes over and their mind begins to drift. It's obvious, isn't it? Well, it's obvious on camera too. Which means you have to really listen to the person who's reading with you. Listen to how they deliver the lines. Listen to which words they emphasis and stress. They might even forget a word or two – which could mean you may have to alter your response slightly for your line to make sense. If you are truly listening, all of this will happen effortlessly.

I am always surprised when actors complain about how casting directors read their lines in an audition. Complaints about a casting director being "monotone", or "not giving me anything" are ridiculous, in my opinion. You are the actor, and you're the one the camera is pointed at. It's up to you to bring the scene to life.

If you go into an audition expecting the other person to read the words in a specific way, you are invariably going to be disappointed. This isn't "paint by numbers". You can't make the other person be what you want them to be, or sound the way you want them to sound. Just as in real life, you have to deal with what you're given.

If the fact that the casting director is not looking at you while she reads her lines bothers you – then get angry! React as you would in real life. If they sound ridiculous – laugh at them! Who cares if the scene isn't written that way? They aren't looking for a mechanical automaton, they want you to be *alive.*

Any literate human being can walk into an audition and recite the lines as they are written. You don't need an actor for that. They want to see whether or not you can bring something more to the party; something they haven't thought of. It might be a look, a reaction, an emotion – or something else altogether. They don't know what they want; that's the whole point. They need you to show them. Don't be afraid to color outside the lines.

And don't be afraid of forgetting your lines. As we learned earlier, often, that's when the best acting takes place. If you draw a complete blank and nothing at all comes, then you need to get really pissed off and look at your script. However, don't read the lines off the script with your head down. Look at your script, get the line, then lift your head up and deliver it. If you're really angry at yourself and emotional because of your mistake – even better.

If you do well in the audition, you may receive a callback. This means you've done your job. An actor who gets callbacks is in the ballgame. If you walked out of the first audition feeling as though you didn't give it your best shot, the callback is your chance to bring something else to the table. Don't throw away what you did the first time, since they obviously liked what they saw. Instead, try to add to it in some small way.

Perhaps develop another transition, or further strengthen the relationship that you have already developed. Don't just assume that because you've gotten a callback, you don't have to prepare anymore. This is a valuable opportunity to fine tune your performance. The more effort you put into it, the better it will be.

ON THE SET

The reason I lumped film and television together into one chapter is because, for an actor, there isn't a significant difference between the two of them. You should prepare and audition for each in exactly the same way. The main difference becomes evident when you show up for work. Television productions are fast-moving affairs. Sometimes, an entire episode can be shot in a single day. By contrast, film productions tend to crawl along at a snail's pace. There are a lot more complicated shots that need to be set up. A single scene in a movie might take days, weeks, or in some extreme instances, months to shoot. Because of that, one of the hardest things about working on the set of a movie is dealing with all the boring downtime.

Showing up on the set of your first feature film can be a little overwhelming. Security and/or crew members will probably be shuttling people around when you arrive. If they try to shove you into the holding area for extras, politely inform them that you are a cast member. After apologizing profusely, they will locate the nearest available PA (Production Assistant) or 2nd AD (Second Assistant Director). You will then be taken to your trailer where you can kick back and relax until wardrobe and makeup are ready to see you.

It's the PA's responsibility to look after the actors and keep track of them. Make sure to let a PA know if you need anything and don't wander too far off without telling them where you're going.

The 2nd AD is responsible for cast notifications, call sheets, production reports, contracts and other documents. This is the person who will probably call you ahead of time to make sure you are up-to-speed with regards to the shoot location, directions and call time.

After you have been through wardrobe and makeup, you will probably have some downtime. More often than not, you will have a lot of it. I've spent twelve hours on a set, ready to go at a moment's notice, only to have my scene postponed until the next day due to failing light. It happens sometimes. Just roll with it. You're being paid to wait, as well as act.

When you finally step onto the set you'll notice a tremendous amount of equipment, activity and people buzzing around. After introductions, the director will walk through the scene to make sure everybody is on the same page with what's happening. Just listen and do as you're told. You will probably do a walkthrough and rehearsal so that the crew can get an idea of how everything is going to look. Then you'll take a break while they set up the lights and equipment. This may take an hour or more.

Once you're called back to set, you will stand on your mark (your starting position) while makeup and wardrobe fuss over you, the sound man hooks you up with a microphone and various other crew members scramble around. Just stay loose and let everybody do their thing.

When everything is ready and the director is finally ready to shoot, a slate will be taken (this is the clapboard which is placed in front of the lens and clapped down). Then the sound man will announce, "Speed" (which means he is recording sound), the camera man will say, "Rolling" (meaning his camera reel is rolling) and the director will say, "Action" which is the signal for the scene to begin.

The scene will play out until the director cries "cut". Sometimes a director will wait and allow a scene to continue in order to see if something develops improvisationally, or for some other reason, so stay in the moment and keep going until the director brings you out.

After you've finished the first take, the director will tell everyone to go, "back to one". This is the signal for everybody to get back into position to start the scene over again. If the cameraman asks to see you on your "end mark", or on your "two position", it simply means that he needs you to move to the spot where you will be standing at the end of the scene. This allows him to set his camera focus on you properly. After he has what he needs, you can go "back to one".

When shooting on the set of a film or television production, one of the most important things for an actor to understand is the need for consistency. In his book *"Audition"*, author Michael Shurtleff felt the topic of consistency was so important that he devoted an entire chapter to the subject. This chapter consists of exactly one sentence: *"Consistency is the death of good acting"*.

What does he mean by that? Well, you have to consider the source and context. Shurtleff is a casting director and he is talking about audition situations. In an audition, casting directors don't want to see the same performance twice. It's a waste of everybody's time. However, there is a world of difference between acting in an audition and acting on the set. When shooting on the set of a movie or TV show, it is absolutely vital for an actor's performances to remain consistent. Here's why:

The first shot is usually a *master*, or *wide shot*. This may cover the entire scene, or parts of it – it all depends on how the director wants to set it up. When you shoot the master, it is extremely important that you pay close attention to what you're doing. Later, you will be expected to match your performance exactly.

After the master has been shot, the director will move the camera in closer for a *two-shot*. As the name suggests, this means there will be two actors visible on the screen at the same time. Once he has the two-shot he will push in closer and focus on one of the actors for a *single*. After he has the single, he will move in to grab a *close-up* and (if he really likes what the actor is doing) perhaps even an *extreme close up* (or ECU).

Once he is satisfied, the director will then flip the set and shoot *reverses*. The camera changes location and the lights are adjusted and focused on the second actor. The process is then repeated with that actor's single, close-up, and (if applicable) ECU. Throughout all of these takes, your performance must remain consistent.

Every film set has someone responsible for continuity. It is the continuity person's job to ensure that the actors' performances remain consistent from take to take. If you are inconsistent, the continuity person will not say a word to you. Instead, he or she will walk over to the director and point out your mistake. The director will then tell you what you are now doing differently from the previous takes, and the scene will have to be shot again. That's if you're lucky.

If you are not so lucky, the continuity person won't spot your mistake. In such cases, the problem may not be discovered until the film goes into post production and the editor begins assembling the scene. If the editor finds that you took off your sunglasses and held them in your right hand in the wide shot, but used your left hand in the two-shot, your time on screen could be significantly trimmed. In a worst-case scenario, it might be cut entirely.

To avoid that, you must be consistent. If you gesture with your hands, you have to remember what gestures you make and on what lines in the dialogue you made them. If you pick up a coffee mug and drink, you need to do it the same way for each take. How are you supposed to remain consistent and yet "in the moment" and "alive" at the same time? Good question!

The answer is, it comes with practice. I don't want you to be overly concerned about this, I just want you to be aware of it. Keep it in the back of your mind. Your main focus shouldn't be on what you're doing with your hands or coffee mug, but on communicating and listening.

When you have finished your last scene and your work on the production is finally complete, the director will announce to everyone on the set that you are officially "wrapped". Upon hearing this, everyone (cast, crew – even the movie stars) will stop whatever they are doing in order to give you a nice round of applause. This is a traditional way of acknowledging your efforts, and recognizing that you are a valuable part of the team – regardless of how small your role was. Take it in stride, and try not to blush too much.

UNIONS: THE SCOOP

There is a lot of confusion surrounding the actor's unions and it isn't just the newbies who are puzzled. Many veteran union members seem confused about policy, details and law. Let's start at the beginning.

First, there are three major actor unions in the United States: *Actors' Equity Association* (AEA) covers live theatre, while all on-camera acting falls under the jurisdiction of either the *Screen Actors Guild* (SAG), or the *American Federation of Television and Radio Artists* (AFTRA).

Once upon a time, life was pretty simple. SAG covered everything shot on film and AFTRA covered TV and radio. Those clearly defined lines began to cross when some productions started shooting television programs and commercials on film. With the development of new media, the jurisdictions have become even more blurred. Today, things break down like this:

Screen Actors Guild (SAG)
- Principal performers in feature motion pictures
- All other types of productions shot on film
- Extra Players in feature motion pictures
- Television programming

- Non-broadcast films and commercials in jurisdiction of:

  – Television programs

  – Television commercials

  – Industrial/educational programs

American Federation of Television and Radio Artists (AFTRA)
- Live television

- Radio programs

- Radio commercials

- Musical recordings

- New technologies like interactive programming and DVD's

- Shares with the S.A.G. video tape jurisdiction for:

  – Television programs

  – Television commercials

  – Industrial/educational programs

- AFTRA represents performer categories such as: Actors, Announcers, Dancers, Disc Jockeys, Newspersons, Singers, Specialty Acts, Sportscasters and Stunt persons.

- AFTRA contracts can also cover Contract and Principal Players, "Under 5's", and Extras.

These days, joining AFTRA is simply a matter of paying the initiation fee. SAG is a little more complicated. In order to be considered for membership in SAG, you must first be cast as a principal in a SAG production, or have been a dues-paying member of one of the other entertainment unions, such as AFTRA, AEA, AGVA (American Guild of Variety Artists), AGMA (American Guild of Musical Artists) or ACTRA (The Canadian Actors Union), for one full calendar year. Once "SAG eligible", you are free to join the guild upon paying the initiation fee.

It's also possible to join SAG by accumulating points doing extra work on SAG productions. However, for reasons stated earlier, if you plan to be a professional actor, extra work is something that I would advise you to stay away from, except in the case of SAG commercials.

When talking about the unions, it's important to know that all states within the U.S. fall into one of two categories: "right-to-work" or "unionized". Basically, in right-to-work states, union affiliation is optional; in unionized states, it isn't.

UNIONIZED STATES

In unionized states, actors are supposed to join the union in order to work in the industry, but there are still quite a lot of non-union productions in unionized states. Non-union actors are free to work in these productions as much and as often as they wish, but once they join any of the three actor unions, they have to stop. Violators risk fines, as well as potential loss of membership.

Since no one is born into the union, every actor begins their career as a non-union actor. Typically, non-union productions pay less than their union counterparts. This is by no means always the case, however. Sometimes a production may be willing to pay considerably more than union scale in exchange for not having to deal with what they perceive as the "hassle" of a union shoot. For the most part though, the biggest productions (and therefore, some of the best acting jobs) tend to fall under union contracts. For this reason, it's probably wise for actors in unionized states to join the unions as soon as possible.

Some people mistakenly believe that non-union actors in unionized states are caught up in a "catch 22" situation, where they can't get a job until they join the guild, but can't join the guild until they get a job. This would have been the case under the old closed shop system. A closed shop is a form of union security agreement in which employers agree to hire only union members. Closed shops were outlawed in the United States in 1947, under the Taft-Hartley Act.

Today, the closed shop has been replaced by the union shop. In a union shop, employers are free to hire both union and non-union members, but non-union employees must agree to join the union within a specified time-frame, or lose their jobs. This is why non-union actors are allowed to audition for union productions in unionized states.

When a non-union actor is hired to be in a production that falls under SAG jurisdiction, a waiver must be applied for. SAG is the only actors union which requires a waiver. This process is nothing more than a formality. Production companies apply for, and are granted waivers by SAG every single day. Once "waivered", the actor is hired under the Taft-Hartley law and immediately becomes "SAG eligible". The actor must then join the union if he intends to continue working on union productions. At least, that's how it works in unionized states.

RIGHT-TO-WORK STATES

In right-to-work states, union shops are illegal. Actors are free to audition and work for any and all productions without ever having to join a union. Strictly speaking, there are no laws prohibiting union members from doing non-union work, but the unions consider such actions to be a violation of their terms of membership, and they reserve the right to punish transgressors accordingly.

For actors who live in right-to-work states, the choice of whether or not to join the unions can be a difficult one. Since the majority of the acting jobs in right-to-work states are often non-union, the financial cost of membership (in terms of jobs lost) can be pretty steep.

A union actor residing in a right-to-work state could miss-out on as much as 80% of the auditions, because in some states, that's how much of the work is non-union. If you're good, that means you could be faced with the stark choice of earning $20,000 per year as a union actor, or $100,000 per year as a non-union actor. When you consider those numbers, it's easy to see why so many actors in right-to-work states remain non-union. And yet, there are still thousands of actors in right-to-work states who do join the unions. Why?

Actually, there are a number of reasons. The first is that many of them simply feel it is the right thing to do. Money isn't everything, and many actors feel a strong loyalty to the unions. Also, some have their sights set on working in New York and L.A. Since both cities are in unionized states, it makes a lot of sense to join the unions before relocating to either of them.

Some actors in right-to-work states join the unions because they are well-established and occasionally book jobs in unionized states. Some join merely so that they can travel out to LA for pilot season (Traditionally, February and March). For these people, it pays to be in the union in order to have a shot at the bigger, out-of-state productions.

There is also a large group of actors who maintain their union memberships simply because they struggled so hard to get them in the first place. These people may work very little (or not at all) throughout the year, but they are proud of what they've accomplished and they enjoy being part of the acting community. They aren't losing out on much work by being in the union, because they wouldn't be working much either way. Many are retired or part-time actors. For these people acting is really a hobby. This is actually true for most union members.

Sometimes in right-to-work states, things can get a little testy between union and non-union actors, but they rarely ever get ugly. The regional communities are mostly too small and tight-knit in order for that to happen. It's perfectly understandable that union members might criticize non-union actors for undermining them, driving down wages, and not paying their dues. It's all true.

Non-union actors counter by pointing out that they're merely operating within the legal system that's in place. They will also claim (correctly) that most union members can afford their idealistic position because acting is either a part-time "hobby" for them, or they are so well-established that they can afford to turn up their noses at the non-union work. Both sides have legitimate points.

So how do we resolve this?

Short of adopting union shop laws in all right-to-work states (which isn't going to happen anytime soon) there isn't a simple answer. However, I think matters would improve if non-union members could at least concede that driving down wages isn't good for anybody.

For that reason (and for reasons that I have stated earlier), we should all agree that actors need to be vigilant about turning down low-paying jobs, and strive to raise our rates. Doing so not only benefits us as individuals, but strengthens the acting community as a whole.

A rising tide lifts all boats. When actors demand higher wages, they are doing their part to raise wages for everybody. They're also increasing their own value in the eyes of industry professionals. How should non-union actors go about demanding higher wages? By asking for them, of course.

As a professional actor, you are going to have to draw a line in the sand and set a minimum standard for yourself sooner or later. When you're just starting out in the business as a non-union actor, it can be tough to know where that line should be drawn. After all, how can you be sure how good you are, or how much you're really worth?

Let me help to get you started by assuring you that you are worth at least union scale. Of course, it's entirely possible (even quite likely) that you could be worth a good deal more than that, but you are certainly not worth less; not unless you are completely devoid of all talent.

Union scale is what everybody in the industry agrees to be minimum wage for actors. In other words, even the penny-pinching, tightwad, "it's not in the budget" producers concede that the worst professional actor in America deserves to be paid at least union scale for his efforts. Scale then, should be considered as the bottom of the barrel. It's the bare-bones minimum.

Knowing that, what shall we say about actors who work for less than union scale? How can they expect to be respected in the industry? How can they be surprised when they're treated poorly on a set or not taken seriously by agents and casting directors?

If you want others to value your talent, you have to value it yourself. Everybody in the business world knows that you don't give away something for nothing. Each time you do a job for less than scale, you're conceding to everyone involved that your acting ability is below par. Sure, by working for less than scale you might make some easy, short-term cash. But it isn't worth it, because the long-term damage to your career and reputation will be devastating.

Not long after I started acting, an agent called me with an interesting proposition. It was a non-union commercial and there was no audition necessary since they had chosen me from my headshot. All I had to do was show up, sit in a convertible sports car and say a couple lines of dialogue. The pay was a thousand dollars.

I was young at the time, and I didn't have much savings. A thousand dollars was nothing to sneeze at. In fact, it would have paid for about three months' rent back then, so it was a significant amount of money. But I turned the job down because I knew it was well below union scale, and I'd decided that scale was my minimum standard.

Did I have any second thoughts? You bet.

They started creeping into my brain just as soon as I hung up the phone. I thought about how hard I'd worked for a thousand dollars in the past, and how long it would have taken me to make that kind of money waiting tables or shucking oysters. I thought about calling my agent back and accepting the job, but I didn't. And you know what? I'm glad I didn't. Because throughout my career, turning down jobs like that has made all the difference. It might be the main reason I've been successful. I certainly believe it has contributed to my success.

I'm not telling you this in order to toot my own horn or hold myself up as some kind of "paragon of virtue". I tell you so that you'll know I understand how hard it can be to walk away from those kinds of gigs. I know it's not easy. But in the long run, it's the best thing for your career.

Have I ever let down my guard and worked for less than I should have? Yes, I'm sorry to say that I have. And I've almost always wound up regretting it. You see, the thing about the easy, low-budget jobs is that all-too-often they turn out to be nightmares. That only makes sense when you consider the reason they're on a tight budget in the first place is because they probably aren't very good at what they're doing. Sometimes they're incompetent, and sometimes it's worse than that.

I have never been "stiffed" on a payment in my life, but I know many actors who have been. It always seems to happen on the low-budget productions, too. If you're going to operate in a right-to-work state without union protection, be careful who you work with. If they cannot afford to pay you properly to begin with, I would avoid them altogether.

UNION BENEFITS

Stories such as these serve to highlight why we have unions in the first place. But there are many benefits to the unions besides setting a minimum standard for pay and seeing to it that we receive our checks. Let's consider some of these now.

Both SAG and AFTRA have health and retirement plans. In each case, you need to work and earn a certain amount of money within one calendar year in order to qualify for insurance. Lately, the minimum amounts needed have been changing regularly so it's best to check their respective websites for the latest info. If you meet the necessary requirements, you are supposed to be notified automatically, but you can check your current status for SAG Pension and Health any time at www.sagph.org. The AFTRA Health & Retirement Fund can be found at www.aftrahr.com.

What's surprising (and confusing) to a lot of people, is that you can both qualify and receive union health and pension benefits without ever actually joining the union. This is because the pension and health plans are entirely separate entities, and distinct from the unions themselves.

When you work under a SAG union contract, for example, the producers contribute 14.3% of your paycheck towards the Producers Pension and Health Plans. Once you reach the SAG Producers Health Plans minimum requirements, the producers have contributed enough in your name for you to fully qualify for coverage, regardless of whether or not you're in the union.

Upon meeting the minimum requirement for health coverage, you will receive a booklet explaining your benefits in detail, as well as your premium amounts. I would advise paying the full premium upfront, if possible. SAG P&H are merciless with late payments and won't hesitate to cancel your coverage if your payment is received even one day late.

Should you qualify for coverage one year and then fail to qualify in the following year, you will be given the option of continuing your coverage under the Self-Pay Program. It's something to consider. The SAG and AFTRA Health plans are probably better than most.

SAG also has an excellent credit union located in Hollywood, CA. If you're a member of the Screen Actors Guild, you should join immediately. It isn't necessary to live in California. Furthermore, once you're a member of the credit union, you're a member for life – even if you retire from SAG. I've financed both my car and my house through the SAG credit union and in both cases they gave me an interest rate which nobody else could even come close to. It's a terrific organization.

Another way in which the unions help actors is by providing standards for work and safety. For example: If you feel that a scene is dangerous, you are within your rights to insist that the production hire a stunt person to take your place. And if you do choose to perform your own stunt, you are entitled to receive extra compensation. You also receive extra compensation for working on weekends and holidays, as well as special dispensations, such as "wet pay" for filming in wet conditions.

There are also strict standards for regular meal times and breaks, and if the shoot doesn't adhere to them, they will have to pay penalties. Similarly, you are to be paid overtime for working over eight hours and you must have at least a 12 hour turnaround (rest time) between shoot days. If you have to travel for the shoot, you must be provided with accommodations, paid per diem and flown 1st class.

KNOW YOUR RIGHTS

Of course, you don't have to be a member of the union in order to demand any of these things. In the business world, all things are negotiable. Unless you're a big-shot, you might have a tough time getting some companies to fly you 1st class (although it never hurts to ask), but at a bare minimum I would always insist upon over-time, travel expenses, per diem, and any other incidentals that might be applicable.

As a professional actor, you should make it your business to be intimately familiar with union contracts, rules and regulations – regardless of whether or not you're a member of the union. You can find out more at:

http://www.sag.org

http://www.aftra.org/home.htm

http://www.actorsequity.org

HOORAY FOR HOLLYWOOD

"Hollywood is a place where they'll pay you a thousand dollars for a kiss and fifty cents for your soul."

- Marilyn Monroe

"Hollywood is where they shoot too many pictures and not enough actors."

- Walter Winchell

Ok. You've done your ground-work in the regional markets and now, at last, you feel you're ready for the big leagues. You wave good-bye to your friends, pack your bags and make the move out to Hollywood. You are confident, because you know what you're doing and you are ready to play. You've learned to run the bases, hit, run, catch, bunt and throw. There's just one, tiny, little problem: As soon as you hit the ground, they hand you a pair of ice skates and a hockey stick and yell, "play ball".

That's how it is, folks. Hollywood is a whole new game.

Much of what you learned in the regional markets does not apply here. Believe every horror story you've ever heard, and then some. This is a tough town. For every actor that "makes it" in Hollywood, there are hundreds of thousands lying by the road. The common belief is that Los Angeles is where actors go to launch their careers. Nothing could be further from the truth. In reality, Los Angeles is where actors go to *bury* their careers. L.A. is a gigantic actor's graveyard.

I know that sounds a tad melodramatic, but that's really how it is. I would love to be able to say that you have a decent chance of making it in Hollywood, but the truth is, you really don't. Nobody does. The odds are gargantuan no matter how talented you are, or how incredibly gorgeous you look. Sorry.

Hollywood is an "all or nothing" deal. You're either in the game, or you're out. There is no in-between. The only real way to get in the game is by being invited to play.

That's not easy, but it is possible if you push your own projects and do good work. By making an award-winning independent film or by hosting your own show on YouTube and generating thousands of subscribers, you might be able to create a situation where Hollywood agents and producers will be interested in hearing what you have to say. However, once you get to that point, you may find that you are no longer interested in what they have to say. If you are really talented, motivated and determined enough to generate your own projects, and those projects are good, then you don't need to worry about kissing anybody's ass. The future is in your hands.

I could talk about this until I'm blue in the face, but I know that no matter what I say, there are going to be a large number of you out there who are still determined to go to Hollywood. Maybe you don't care about the odds. Maybe you are convinced that you are destined for greatness. Who knows? Maybe you are. I am not trying to rain on your parade; I am just trying to provide you with a realistic assessment of the situation, so you will have some idea of what you are getting yourself into. Your chances of making it as an actor in Hollywood are similar to your chances of winning the lottery. Maybe not even that good.

On the other hand, it is an undeniable fact that some people do win the lottery, and it's also true that you can't win unless you play. I guess I've made my point. If you're still determined to take your shot at "Tinsel Town", then so be it. All that remains is for me to tell you how to maximize your chances of success.

GETTING YOUR FOOT IN THE DOOR

The first thing you should know about Hollywood is that agents are very suspicious of non-L.A. area codes. Query letters that contain contact information with out-of-town addresses and strange area codes tend to be tossed in the garbage. Therefore, before you physically move out there, you want to make it really easy for them to get back in touch with you.

If you reside outside of the Los Angeles area, the first thing you need to do is obtain a local L.A. number, or set up an 800 number to use as your main contact number. Shop around for the best deals online. Be sure to include your email address in the letter, of course. For some agents, this will be their preferred method of contacting you.

You will want to arrange interviews with both talent agents and managers. The goal is to have a string of meetings set up and ready to go as soon as you step off the plane. Start by visiting www.samuelfrench.com and grab the latest issue of *"Personal Managers (Los Angeles)"*, by Keith Wolfe. This will give you a wealth of valuable information on L.A. managers, as well as their updated addresses.

When sending out your packages, I recommend that you send a proper package via snail mail as opposed to using email. It comes across as more professional. Agents, like most of us, are constantly bombarded with unsolicited emails and most simply refuse to compound the problem by accepting them from new talent. Of course, since email is free, you can always take your chances and give it a shot. However, you do run the risk of making yourself look like an ass. Unsolicited emails (even when they are read) just don't make a great first impression.

Send packages with your headshot and a cover letter to 30 or 40 agents and managers. Keep the cover letter brief and to the point. No pleading, begging and groveling if you please. That just makes you look pathetic. Keep it succinct. You're addressing fellow professionals about a business matter. There's no room for frills or cutesy stuff here. Just introduce yourself, and give them a brief rundown of what you've been doing recently. Tell them you're moving to L.A. and specify on which date you're going to be available for an interview. You should expect to wait anywhere from one to three weeks for a response. If you don't get any responses after three weeks, send out another mailer.

One more thing: In your letter (and later, in your interview) it's extremely important that you never give the impression that you're "just visiting", or simply "checking things out" (even if that's exactly what you are doing). Hollywood agents and managers don't have time to cater to tourists. You have to give them the impression that you are serious, and that you're going to be sticking around for the long haul.

MANAGERS

Everybody knows that to be successful in L.A., an actor has to have an agent. But opinions vary as to whether or not managers are necessary. Even though the functions of managers can cross paths with agents on occasion, managers are really very different from agents. For a start, managers take more of your paycheck. While an agent takes 10%, managers usually charge 15%. Some go higher than that.

Unlike agents, managers tend to take more of a hands-on approach with their actors that agents simply don't have time for. This might include giving feedback on hairstyle and clothes in order to build up a certain image or distinctive "look". In some cases (and especially in the case of stars), it might even go so far as running errands for the actor, or picking up relatives at the airport!

For the most part, it's an agent's job to get you auditions and nego-tiate your contract. The manager's job is to market you, but sometimes managers get you auditions, too. L.A. managers are in the business of managing talent because they know lots of people who are influential in the business. In the dog-eat-dog, what have you done for me lately world of L.A. – that's the sort of person you want to have on your side.

In my opinion, a good manager is absolutely vital in Hollywood – especially when you're just starting out. With a manager, you can make contacts in a matter of weeks that would have otherwise taken years. That's important. When you are an L.A. actor, you're not just competing with a million other actors, you are racing against the clock.

In Hollywood, if you're a child actor, it's forgivable that you haven't starred in a major production. After all, you're just a kid. But by the time you reach the mid-to-late 20's, inexperience isn't so read-ily excusable. Somewhere around your mid 20's, your acting cred-ibility will begin to suffer if you are not booking acting roles. It will continue to drop with each passing year until you start booking. The longer you go without work in L.A., the harder it becomes to get work in L.A. Thus, the vicious cycle. With each passing year, your plight becomes ever more desperate. That's why one of the first sentences out of every Hollywood agent's mouth is always going to be, "So… what have you been working on recently?"

It's pretty difficult to go more than two years in Hollywood without booking a role and expect anybody to take you seriously as an actor. Los Angeles is full of would-be actors that haven't had a role in years. Some go ten years or more without landing an agent or manager! Yet they sit around hoping that one day, their ship will come in. They are kidding themselves. Please, don't let that happen to you. Zero work means zero credibility. In Hollywood, no credibility means no chance.

So yes, you will need a manager. Anyone who can build momen-tum for you is someone you want on your team. How can you be sure that you have what Hollywood agents and managers are looking for?

Well, you can't. You're just going to have to submit your headshot and find out for yourself. The truth is, whether you succeed or fail in Hollywood is largely going to be out of your hands. It's up to others to decide whether you are marketable or not.

Everything will depend on what you have to offer, and what agents and managers happen to be looking for at the time. If you've just played a major role in a hit Broadway show, or starred in a successful feature film, you can feel pretty good about your chances of generating some interest. If you've recently graduated from a major drama program, it will be a big feather in your cap and you should have a fairly good shot of setting up some appointments. If you are extraordinarily beautiful, or a highly unusual physical type, such as Verne Troyer or Richard Kiel, you may generate some interest based solely on your appearance. In all cases, youth always works in your favor. What I mean by that is, the younger you are, the less your lack of experience counts against you.

Updated contact information for talent agencies in Hollywood can be obtained from *Call Sheet*. Last time I checked, you could get a copy at www.samuelfrench.com for about $10.

Mailings to talent agents follow the same rules as managers. Include your headshot, resume and a cover letter. Keep the letter brief and stress that you are in the process of moving to LA. Let them know that you want to set up an interview to discuss representation. Give them three or four weeks to get back to you. If you don't hear from them by then, you probably never will. But don't worry, that isn't the end of the world.

START YOUR OWN ENGINE

*"Make mistakes of ambition and not mistakes of sloth.
Develop the strength to do bold things, not to suffer."*
- Niccolo Machiavelli

Ok, you finally arrive and settle into your new surroundings. You meet with some agents and managers and (hopefully) list with a couple of them. Now what?

Most actors go to Hollywood with a game plan of sorts. This usually involves trolling the beaches, bars and party scene trying to look cool and sexy. The hope is that they'll eventually bump into someone famous who will be immediately struck by their talent and big screen potential. In this way, they will get their much-deserved "big break".

If you've been paying attention at all up until now, I don't have to explain why this is a really bad plan. Once again, following the majority of actors is a sure-fire recipe for disaster.

No one is going to spot you in a grocery store and give you top billing in a Hollywood movie. It just doesn't work like that. Maybe it happened a few times in the 1920's and 30's, but not anymore. Movies today cost a lot of money. That means you need investors. Investors hate risk. Unknown actors are very, very, risky. This is why you see the same faces on television and in films over and over again. It isn't necessarily because these actors are so much better than everybody else, it's just that they are known quantities (and their risk is therefore limited).

A reputation is essential in Hollywood. Even a bad one is better than nothing at all! Therefore, you're going to have to create a reputation for yourself. I'll assume you'd prefer to be known for your talent rather than with whom you sleep, so we'll concentrate on what you can do to develop a good reputation as a talented actor.

Where to start? There is almost no live theatre in L.A., making the route most logical in any other city almost impossible here. Again, this is why a good manager is so vital in Los Angeles. A good manager can get you in front of casting directors. Of course, once in front of them, it's entirely up to you to blow their doors off with your performance.

You will see a lot of classes and workshops advertised in Los Angeles, but proceed with caution. There's an enormous cottage industry here that survives on the blood, sweat and tears of wide-eyed wannabes who have just moved to the big city. Don't behave as if you've just fallen off of the turnip truck. Be wary of scams and study your options carefully.

If you really want give yourself a fighting chance, there's no better way to do it than by starting your own project. This is good advice for any actor, regardless of where in the world you happen to live, but it's never truer than in Hollywood.

Write something. It could be a screenplay, sketch comedy, stand-up routine, anything. Write it with yourself in mind and use it as a vehicle to further your career. If you don't know what to write, ask yourself what your dream role would be. Think big. Once you've come up with something, don't sit around waiting for that scenario to fall into your lap. Make it happen!

Do not go to Hollywood hoping to be discovered. You want to go there first and foremost with the intention of getting your project off the ground. Your acting career needs to be a secondary consideration (at least as far as everyone you meet is concerned).

This entails making a small mental shift in priorities, but that shift will make all the difference in your state of mind, as well as the impression you will make on everyone you meet. Nobody in Hollywood wants to meet another lazy, unemployed, wannabe actor. Everybody in Hollywood wants to meet a person who is writing, producing and/ or directing a great new project that might have something in it for *them*. Remember that.

If you aren't a good writer, then collaborate with someone who is. Seek out and make friends with the people you need in order to move your project along. Hollywood isn't about strolling down the beach waiting to be discovered, it's about pushing projects, shaking hands, doing lunch and cutting deals. That is the game. If it isn't the game you want to play, then you are in the wrong town.

But what if you don't have any projects, or even any ideas for projects? After all, you're an actor, not a writer or a director.

That's fair enough. Here's what I want you to do: Spend some time thinking about what would be the perfect role for you. Really think about it. Don't worry about a plot or anything at this point, just concentrate on a character that you could do well. Ideally, it should be something that you think you could do better than anybody else. Once you have that, it's simply a matter of creating a story around that character. That's how Sylvester Stallone came up with the character of "Rocky". It's what Matt Damon and Ben Affleck did with "Good Will Hunting." Both films won Oscars, and both were launching pads for the actors involved.

Had they never written their own material or pushed their own projects, people such as Owen and Luke Wilson, Tina Fey, Seth Rogen, Will Ferrell, Jon Favreau, Steve Martin, Billy Bob Thornton, Ellen DeGeneres, Adam Sandler, Mike Myers, Chris Rock, Jackie Chan, Wanda Sykes, Jay Leno, Ben Affleck, Carol Burnett, Dan Aykroyd, John Cleese, Michael Palin, Ricky Gervais, Tyler Perry, Larry David, Ed Burns, Jerry Seinfeld and many, many others would still be completely unknown to you and just about everybody else on the planet.

The people who succeed in Hollywood are, by and large, the people who generate their own work and push their own projects. Not easy to do, but easy to understand.

Why sit around waiting for someone to cast you in a role that's tailor made for you, when you can come up with the role on your own and tailor it to yourself? That's a pretty good way to guarantee you get the part.

One more thing: When you're brainstorming and trying to come up with a project – think big. A common mistake among young film-makers is going "low budget". It makes sense that when you're starting out you should start out small. But the truth is that in Hollywood, it's actually a lot easier to raise money for the big projects than for the little ones. That may sound counter-intuitive, but if you think about it, it makes perfect sense. Nobody wants to be part of a low-budget production. I know I don't. They're a pain in the butt. But *everybody* wants to be part of a big-budget production. There's more money, more visibility, more credibility – more everything. So don't waste your time trying to put together a low budget movie. Every resource you need, writers, directors, producers, crew, talent – they're all around you in Hollywood. Most of them are out of work and looking for something to do. Use them! Think big and aim high.

Even if your film never comes to fruition, simply coming up with an idea for a project is a great way to make friends and build connections with other people in the industry. Who knows where that could lead? Furthermore, creating your own project gives you something to focus on besides auditions (which you may or may not be getting). Remember, you never want to present yourself as a desperate, starving actor. When an industry pro asks you what you're working on, you need to be able to say something more impressive than, "my tan".

How much time should you give yourself to succeed in Holly-wood? That's a tough question. It's your life, and in the end, only you can say. The general consensus seems to be that it's going to take one to two years just to get settled in before you can reasonably expect to make any headway.

Give yourself some time to get up to speed. It is going to take a while. Take charge of your career. Hammer the agents and managers.

Sell them on why they need to work with you. Show them how you're going to make them money. Then, when you sign with them, don't just sit around waiting for the phone to ring. Collaborate with others. Feed off of their energy and creativity. Develop your own projects. That's how you play the Hollywood game.

THE "Q" FACTOR

"I had an epiphany a few years ago where I was out at a celebrity party and it suddenly dawned on me that I had yet to meet a celebrity who is as smart and interesting as any of my friends."
- Moby

The last thing that I want to mention about Hollywood is something called the "Q" Factor – or "Q" rating system. It's rather peculiar, and most people have never heard of it, but it's an important piece of the puzzle when it comes to understanding how Hollywood works.

The "Q" rating system was created by Marketing Evaluations/TvQ Inc., of New York. It tracks and measures the appeal of individual actors, TV shows and movies. Every actor who has appeared on film or television has a "Q" score. This can be used by executives as a bargaining tool to decide what gets picked up for the coming season, or as an indicator to gauge the popularity of a star, and perhaps, the potential revenue of a project.

The system is supposed to be fairly complex, but generally speaking, the more recognizable the face, the higher their "Q" score will be. Remember how credibility trumps talent in the acting world (at least, as far as producers are concerned)? In Hollywood, visibility is credibility. That's how it's possible for someone like Shakil O'Neal to be cast as the lead in a major movie, and Paris Hilton to have her own TV show, while most of Broadway's top actors will never be considered for either one. That, in a nutshell, is Hollywood. It isn't about who you know; it's all about who knows you.

THE BIG APPLE

If you dream of making it big in the daytime soaps, commercials or musical theatre, then New York City could be the place for you. As you might imagine, all three of these fields are insanely competitive. What's more, the line from the old Sinatra song, "...If I can make it there, I'll make it anywhere..." doesn't ring true anymore. Success on Broadway no longer guarantees stardom in the way it once did.

Many actors go to New York with the intention of using it as a stepping stone for Hollywood; their theory being that it is somewhat easier to get established in New York before making the move out west. In my opinion, this is a big mistake. If Hollywood is your ultimate goal, then I advise you to pack your bags and get out there as soon as possible. "Making it" in New York isn't significantly easier than "making it" in Hollywood. Building credibility in the Big Apple will almost certainly take years of hard work. With each passing day, you will grow a little older and lose valuable time. Remember, in Hollywood, "youth" is one of your most marketable assets. Agents and managers in L.A. are far more willing to take a chance on a promising new talent if that talent also happens to be young. It's simply a matter of economics. The younger you are, the more time and potential you have.

Of course, if you're also well trained, that's even better; and there's the rub. In order to maximize your chances of success, it helps to be well trained at a young age. New York has plenty of opportunities for great training. The acting programs at NYU and Julliard are two of the most highly regarded in the world, but there are also a myriad of workshops and ongoing classes that you could take. Many of these will pit you up against some of the finest talent this country has to offer. Of course, the same can be said for Los Angeles.

If you're going to live and work in New York City, I recommend that you take time out to audition for the Actors' Studio. The Actors' Studio is a non-profit organization for professional actors. You have to be 18 or older in order to audition (as well as have some background training and/or experience as an actor). But if you make it through the audition process, admission to the studio is free, and it's good for life. The Actors' Studio isn't a school (although they do endorse an MFA program in conjunction with Pace University); it is a studio where actors can go to develop material and work on honing their skills. Think of it as a membership-run gymnasium for professional actors. It's a great place to spread your wings and perhaps even make some valuable contacts. You can find out more information at www.theactorsstudio.org. The Actors' Studio now also has a branch in West Hollywood.

New York has one big advantage over Hollywood in that it affords you the opportunity to work on the stage. As with the regional markets, this is where you have a chance to stand out from the pack and show what you can do. Of course, that isn't going to be nearly as easy here as it would be in the smaller markets, but if you really think you have what it takes to compete with the best, this is your chance to prove it.

On the whole, New York talent agents are true professionals. Many of them make a point of taking time out of their daily lives to attend plays, experimental theatre and showcases in the hopes of spotting hot new talent. When you're on the stage in New York, you must always take care to do your best work. There's no telling who might be sitting in the audience watching you perform on any given night.

DAYTIME SOAPS

Breaking into daytime soaps is a major point of focus for many New York actors. The hours on a soap can be brutal and relentless. In the old days, productions would have TelePrompTers set up all over the set so that actors could refer to them if they got stuck. Unfortunately, actors began to get lazy and started reading all of their lines off the prompters. This became so obvious after a while that the TelePrompTers were removed altogether. Nowadays, soap actors often have to power-memorize masses of lines in a very short amount of time. That isn't easy, but I suppose it is good training.

If the soaps hold a special allure for you, then the first thing you need to do is pick up a copy of *Call Sheet* (formerly known as the *Ross Reports*). *Call Sheet* is published monthly. It lists casting directors, independent casting companies, talent agents and casting personnel at prime-time television series and soaps in both New York and LA. You can get a copy at www.samuelfrench.com. What you're interested in are the specific casting directors that cast the major soaps.

Contrary to what many actors will tell you, you do not have to have an agent in order to submit yourself to a casting director. Anybody can put together a package and submit themselves. Packages should include a headshot, resume and a short cover letter. In the cover letter, tell them what you're currently working on (e.g. classes you have recently completed, jobs that you were booked on or called back for, showcases you will be appearing in, etc...).

As always, keep your letter short and to the point. A paragraph or two is plenty. You can send packages to the same people over and over again (once every three to four weeks is enough to seem persistent without becoming a nuisance); however, every time you send a package it's going to be important for you to include new information. You need to be showing them that you are making progress in some facet of your career. Don't just blindly send the same letter over and over again. If you have nothing new to say, then there's no reason to send a package.

Don't bother trying to harass agents into seeing you. It will never work. The only way to get their attention is by showing them that you're making headway in your career. If you find that you are going months without making any progress worth mentioning, then you're not working hard enough. You need to get busy.

One more thing: When you write to the casting directors just say you'd like to work with them, don't mention extra work. You need to be thinking big. Behave as if you know you're going to be a major player. If they come back and offer you a role as an extra, you should probably go ahead and take it. Just make sure it's their idea, not yours. Don't act grateful and overjoyed about it, either (at least not to them). Extra work on a soap opera is about as prestigious as cleaning the toilets, but it does get your foot in the door.

As I've stated repeatedly, New York soaps and S.A.G. commercials are the only two instances where I think it's permissible for you to do extra work. There is a small chance that you could be singled out on the set of a soap opera and given a larger role. It has been known to happen, on occasion. Of course, this assumes that you are extremely good-looking. Getting noticed as an extra on a soap has absolutely nothing to do with your acting ability. Extras never get the opportunity to act.

Extra work is nothing for you to be proud of, so if you are going to do it, don't advertise it. Never use extra work as a reason to send a cover letter to anybody and don't even think about putting it on your resume. Extra work undermines your credibility as an actor. Therefore, it is counter-productive to what you are ultimately trying to achieve.

COMMERCIALS IN NEW YORK

Manhattan is the Mecca of big-time commercials. If you've worked consistently in the regional markets and have built up a decent demo reel, you might have a legitimate shot at launching a successful commercial career in New York City. Commercials are big money in the Big Apple, and a good one could be worth a king's ransom.

Again, this is a long shot. Keep in mind that you are exchanging the consistent, smaller work of the regional markets for the possibility of hitting a grand slam home run in the majors.

Paul Marcarelli is one of my heroes. Chances are, you probably don't know the name, but I have no doubt that you would instantly recognize his face. Paul is the unassuming, bespectacled front man for the *Verizon* commercials which have been running on television for about a decade now. For the first few years, Paul walked around saying, "Can you hear me now? Can you hear me now?" Lately, he just stands with an unassuming look on his face, wearing black glasses and a grey coat, flanked by hundreds of extras.

I don't know how much *Verizon* pays Paul (it's a negotiated contract and confidential), but it has got to be in the seven-figure range. In fact, it may be around seven figures *per commercial*. Regardless of the actual number, Paul shouldn't be strapped for cab fare any time soon.

That is the sort of thing that can happen in the New York City commercial market. Jobs like Paul's *Verizon* gig don't come around every day, or even every year, but they do come around. And it only takes one.

So what's the downside?

If acting in Hollywood is like playing the lottery, then New York is a little bit like panning for gold; do it long enough and there's a chance you'll find some nice-sized nuggets. You might even get lucky, strike a vein and make your millions.

But how long will it take you to accomplish that? Ten years? Twenty? The truth is, no matter how long your time horizon happens to be, the odds are still going to be against you, simply because there's so much competition.

On the other hand, if you're good enough to "play ball" in New York, then I can confidently say that your chances of earning a million dollars in the regional markets over a ten-year period are pretty darned good. I know, because I've done it. Will I do it again over the next decade? Obviously, I can't say for sure, but I like my chances. It's just so much easier making a consistent living hitting singles in the minors, than it is swinging for home runs in the majors. There may be less glory, but there is a lot more consistency. It's also easier to live a normal life (house, car, family) and enjoy a higher standard of living.

In the end, it isn't so much about one path being right or wrong; it's about the kind of life you prefer. Some people adore living in New York City and being in the middle of all that action. More power to them. As far as I'm concerned, it's a nice place to visit.

Even if commercial acting in the Big Apple sounds like your kind of game, it still makes a lot of sense for you to start out in the regional markets. Build up your video reel, join the unions and get some real-world experience under your belt, then make your move. All of that shouldn't take you much more than a year; two at the most. During this "prep" time, you can also save some money. You'll need plenty of it in Manhattan.

Once you've learned the ropes and joined the unions, send out a package of headshots and demo reels to the major commercial agencies in New York, along with a short cover letter. Tell them that you are an experienced commercial actor who is already in the unions, and that you would like to meet with them to discuss representation. You don't need a drama degree (or any other kind of degree) in order to land a top commercial agent in New York City. You just have to look marketable and be able to convince the agents that you know what you're doing.

Theatrical agents are a completely different matter altogether.

Theatrical agents are going to want to see a proven track record (on the stage, screen or both). Failing that, you will at least need to show them that you've made it through a highly-regarded drama program. These are minimum requirements. If you don't meet them, then you need to start working towards them. Take classes, hone your abilities and build your resume with the goal of obtaining theatrical representation at some point in the future. Meanwhile, if you can support yourself with commercial work (or at least supplement your income with it), so much the better.

And who knows? There's always the off-chance that you could strike it rich by landing a terrific ad campaign. In such an instance, you might quickly find yourself in a situation where, almost overnight, agents and managers on both coasts are clamoring to represent you.

THE PROBLEM WITH A NEW YORK STATE OF MIND

I like New York actors a lot. For the most part, they take their work seriously and strive to be the best that they can be. Unlike many wannabe movie-stars on the West Coast, New York actors are prepared to work for success rather than wait around for a hand-out. No one is more conscious of that fact than N.Y. actors themselves, and they take pride in it. This is why you will often hear them refer to the business of acting as, *The Craft*. They call it a craft because, much like a carpenter or blacksmith, they recognize that an actor's skills need to be developed and refined over time. There's a lot to be said for that way of thinking. In fact, it's the same thing I've been preaching all along.

So what's the problem?

Part of it has to do with the city itself. It's hard, fast, expensive, and competitive as hell. It wears you down. When I first started out as an actor in Atlanta, I booked an average of one job for every four auditions that I went out on. When I moved up to New York, that rate dropped to one job in every 35 to 40 auditions. And believe it or not, my agency considered that to be an excellent percentage.

What was worse, the jobs I was landing weren't paying me much more than the ones I had been booking in Atlanta. Add to that the fact that the cost of living in New York was twice as high and my apartment was half as big, and you begin to get an idea of the dismal, overall picture. Small wonder that after years of essentially, "auditioning for a living", many New York actors tend to become a little bit jaded.

Another issue has to do with acting instructors. As I mentioned earlier, many insist on pushing the idea that actors are artists. They do it because it sounds good, sells well, and in some cases, maybe they actually believe it.

It's nonsense, and it needs to stop.

It is possible for a blacksmith or a carpenter to reach a level of craftsmanship where, in time, they might be considered as an artist (or artisan), but that doesn't happen overnight.

Yet, many New York actors seem to be under the impression that the instant they decide to become actors, they immediately morph into artists that same afternoon. If actors such as Marlon Brando and Paul Newman go out of their way to avoid the label of "artist", what right does any actor have to lay claim to that title? It is as preposterous as it is pretentious. It's also bad for business.

When an actor considers himself to be an artist, everything becomes *personal.* Each time he loses out on an audition, he feels rejected. When his work is criticized, it stings all that much more because it is his art, his very *soul* that is being trampled upon. At least, that's how it feels...

Why put yourself through all of that?

It is so much healthier to think of yourself as a businessperson, or even as a product, not much different than those sold by Coke, IBM or Apple. I know it isn't as sexy, but it is more accurate. Talent agents, managers and producers will certainly be thinking of you in those sort of business terms. Why not be on the same page as them from the beginning?

When you think of yourself as a business owner with a product or service for sale, you take your ego out of the equation. Criticism becomes nothing more than customer feedback. When you lose out on an audition, it isn't a matter of your talent being rejected; you just didn't make a sale, that's all. It's business. It's nothing personal.

Corporations spend millions of dollars on customer feedback, and not all of that feedback is good. When it's bad, the executives don't curl up into a ball and moan about how no one appreciates their artistic genius. They don't waste time burying their heads in the sand. They face up to it, and try to learn from it. They go back to the drawing board and have open, honest discussions. They try to figure out where they went wrong.

Instead of searching for cheap compliments to help patch their self-esteems, they try to get honest feedback so that they can accurately assess the product's shortcomings. They work hard to figure out what they can do better, then they take all of that information and use it to refine, adapt and improve their product.

You are running a business too, and you're getting customer feedback every time you audition – whether you like it or not. If you aren't making sales (getting callbacks; booking jobs), you need to be taking that information and using it to figure out a way to develop and improve your product – just as Coke, Apple, and IBM would do. You may need to work on marketing, training, credibility, your physical appearance or all of the above. Figure out where you are weak and get to work on it.

When you approach acting as a business, failures, criticisms and rejections turn into valuable lessons. Instead of allowing yourself to become insulted and depressed by them – face them and embrace them! It might sound corny, but that's how empires are built.

If you live in New York for any length of time, sooner or later you are going to run into unemployed actors laboring under the delusion that they are gifted, misunderstood, and unappreciated artists. Don't allow these people to drag you down into their way of thinking. It's hard enough making a living in New York City as it is, without burying yourself under a mountain of self-pity.

Keep your chin up, stay humble and remain positive. Stick to the mantra that you are a marketable product rather than an artist, and you will profit as a result.

FAME

"A celebrity is someone who works hard all his life to become well-known, then wears dark glasses to avoid being recognized."
- Fred Allen

"If you don't believe the legend... then you can't really take yourself seriously. And if you don't take yourself seriously, you've got a chance. It's when you take yourself seriously and you begin to believe all this bullshit that you can really founder."
- Paul Newman

I don't think an acting book can be considered complete without mentioning a few words about the subject which drives so many of us into this business in the first place. By now, you should realize that fame is not a prerequisite for acting success. Nor is it always a byproduct of it. You can have a terrific career as an actor without ever being famous; and yet, I don't think it's a stretch to say that all actors dream of attaining fame at some point in their lives. It's easy to imagine why. Fame is the ultimate stamp of success. It promises job security, respect, recognition and wealth. It also comes with a few downsides.

We all know (or think we know) the dangers and pitfalls of fame:

The pressure of always having to look your best; the complete loss of privacy; the risk of being stalked or targeted by some nutcase. Is it really worth it? Millions seem to think so.

Contrary to the lyrics of Irene Cara's hit song, fame does not mean that you're going to live forever. In fact, it's rare for an actor's fame to last much beyond his or her own lifetime. And for the legendary few who do manage to remain household names long after they have passed away, it's simply a question of time before their names fade from the public's memory as well.

How many actors can you name from 100 years ago? How many of those do you really know anything about? The silent film era had mega stars the likes of which can hardly be equaled today. Yet now, all of their loves, lives, personalities – even their films are, for the most part, long forgotten. All glory is fleeting. However, unlike a great many writers, painters and poets, at least famous actors get to enjoy the fruits of their labor while they are still alive. I suppose there is something to be said for that.

The desire for fame can be a driving force that pushes you to excel and achieve. When it does, I think it's probably a good thing. In fact, anything that motivates us to get up of the couch and move around is probably a good thing. I won't spend much time talking about the benefits of fame, because they're pretty obvious. There is another side of the coin, however, and it is an aspect we would be foolish to overlook.

THE EMPEROR SYNDROME

"Adversity makes men, and prosperity makes monsters."

- Victor Hugo

At the beginning of this book, I talked about how most successful actors have engaging personalities and make terrific first impressions. It's true. The overwhelming majority are delightful to be around. And yet, everybody knows that fame has a way of changing people. It is an undeniable fact that many superstars develop massive egos and insufferable personalities. Why? What happens to them?

When you first start out as an actor in the movies, or on television, it's surprising how much you're pampered. Absolutely everything is handled for you. Someone puts on your makeup and someone else does your hair. Your clothes are washed and pressed each day. PA's are ready and willing to fetch you a drink, food, a chair – anything you need. You are waited on hand and foot and you don't even have to tip anybody. It's wonderful.

The first time I experienced this sort of royal treatment I thought, "I could really get used to this." And after the first few days, I did get used to it. Before long, I began to expect it. Unfortunately, my time on the set ended after only a couple of weeks and then I had to return home. I was soon back to washing my own laundry and cooking my own meals. Back to reality.

But what if I had been the star of the movie? In that case, there would have been no "back to reality". Reality would have been the life of an emperor. And that's exactly how most stars are treated. It only stands to reason that if everyone treats you like an emperor, sooner or later, you're going to begin to act like one. When that happens, you are one short step away from *demanding* to be treated like an emperor.

Take that final step, and you have officially crossed over to the dark side.

Some stars can't help but take that final step. I'm not going to name any names, or point any fingers. Nor can I say that I would act any differently than them under similar circumstances. Based on my brief experiences on film sets, I'm inclined to think I wouldn't behave any differently at all. Nevertheless, stories abound of film and television personalities whom the public adores, but everyone in the industry despises. Often, these people manage to get away with selfish and insufferable behavior for years. Occasionally, they expose and embarrass themselves publicly, but for the most part, their behavior is quickly overlooked and forgiven. As long as they are hot, everyone puts up with it. They might not like it, but they put up with it. Fame is fleeting, however, and when the tide turns there are those who take great pleasure in ensuring that these megalomaniacs crash back down to reality. Hard.

For the former star, it often means an ignominious, and occasionally tragic ending. Many turn to drugs or alcohol. Some might take it as far as suicide. As the old saying goes, "The bigger they are, the harder they fall." Perhaps the only thing worse than going through something like that, is going through it while the whole world watches.

That's where we don't want to end up: Trapped in a fish-bowl of our own making, while the world sits back and watches us self-destruct. There is only one way to ensure that we avoid it. We have to get our priorities straight right from the beginning. We have to stay humble.

Beyonce Knowles told Britain's Daily Telegraph a story about a public altercation that she had with her mother inside a record store. It's a great example of what I'm talking about. Here it is in her own words:

"When I was 19 — when I was confused and wondering what am I doing, who am I? — we were in the record store, my mom and dad were both there, and my song was playing, and I was feeling like hot stuff.

She was asking me something and I started singing while she was talking to me. And there were some really cute guys in the store who were noticing me, and I was like, 'Oh yeah! I'm hot!' And my mom said, 'I'm talking to you'. And I kept singing. And so she smacked me — slapped me in my face, so hard.

And my dad said, 'What are you doing?' Because I didn't get spankings growing up. They didn't believe in that. My mom says, 'She thinks she's hot stuff because her single is out. You are still my child. Now go sit in the car'.

But it was the best thing she could have ever done to me because for the first time I realized I was losing sight of what was important."

Recently, in an interview on NPR, Beyonce was asked about this incident again. She admitted that it was horribly embarrassing for her at the time, but looking back now, she credits her mom with literally saving her life. I give her a lot of credit for seeing the big picture here. Most people would have been so caught up in their own anger and shame that they would have missed that lesson entirely. I'm sure I wouldn't have been as wise when I was nineteen.

Whether or not you become famous, it's going to be important for you to keep your ego in check and your career in proper perspective. In the acting world, that's easier said than done. When we work, we are surrounded by people who treat us like royalty. When we're not working, we spend a lot of time focusing on ourselves. Under such conditions, how can anyone maintain their sanity for long?

The first thing you need to understand (and what you must constantly remind yourself), is that all of this fuss really isn't about you at all. If you're making a movie, it's about the characters and the story. When you shoot a commercial, it is the product that is the hero. Even if you become a celebrity and find yourself standing on a red carpet among a throng of adoring fans and flashing bulbs, even then, it isn't so much about you, as the product you have become, and the industry that has been created around you. It's about selling magazines, newspapers, theatre seats, DVD's, toys, games, and commercial air-time. It's about *the machine*, and the large group of individuals who are making money off of your name and image. Not you.

If you expect to keep that machine running, it's going to be important for you to keep your ego in check.

Success demands humility.

GET A LIFE

"I didn't devote my life to acting. I give a lot to my work, but my life has always been more important."
- Catherine Deneuve

"I don't think being a movie star is a good enough reason for existing."
- Natalie Wood

Occasionally, I post on various acting forums online in order to help any struggling actors willing to listen to what I have to say. A few years ago, I found myself corresponding with a young woman living in Holland. She was having a tough time in the business and wanted some advice. I asked her to tell me about her situation and from all outward appearances she seemed to have her ducks in row. She struck me as intelligent, articulate and (judging by her headshot) attractive.

At first, I wasn't really sure what to tell her. Then she made an interesting and rather revealing comment; "If I cannot act, I don't know what I will do. I don't even have a boyfriend. Acting is my whole life."

Got it. Mystery solved.

So I wrote back, and this is what I said:

"In my opinion, you're putting far too much emphasis on acting. I think you should take a step back and forget about it for a while. Treat yourself to a nice vacation for a couple of weeks. Make it longer if you can afford it. Go somewhere you've never been. You need to challenge yourself and expand your horizons. Be adventurous! Choose a country where you do not speak the native language.

When you throw yourself into these sorts of situations, it forces you out of your comfort zone and you have no choice but to open up. Once you do, you will find that people really are friendly and helpful — especially when you don't speak their language. It's amazing how well you can communicate with someone when neither of you understands a word the other is saying. That in itself is a valuable acting lesson.

Immerse yourself in the local culture. Eat their food, adopt their customs and try to learn a bit of their language. Even if you struggle, they'll love you for trying. Of course, many things will be strange and scary, but that's the whole point! You are going to make new friends and have all sorts of crazy adventures. Be sure to take a camera with you. It's a great ice-breaker. Sing with the locals, drink their wine, and dance whenever you can.

If you can muster the courage to do this, I guarantee you will come back a better actor. It will probably be a life-changing experience for you. Who knows? You might even fall in love."

She thanked me, told me it was the best advice she'd ever received and said that she would definitely do as I suggested. I wish I could tell you that she went on to become a great actress, but the truth is, I don't know what happened to her. I never heard from her again. Maybe she met the love of her life and got married... or, maybe she was ship-wrecked and eaten by cannibals. I have no idea.

Either way, I like to think her world became a little less boring. When a person devotes their whole life to acting, they are making a tragic mistake. Not only are they missing out on all the wonderful things life has to offer, they're actually *inhibiting* their chances of ever having a successful acting career. It's a strange dichotomy, and here again, it's the opposite of what you might expect. However, if you think about it, it makes perfect sense.

Here's why:

If you want to be an Olympic athlete, you're going to have to train hard to ensure you are faster, stronger or more skillful than your competition. In order to do that, you will probably have to make train-ing your main focus for a number of years. Family, friends, personal vacations – everything else in your life will have to take a back seat. The same is true for a concert pianist, middleweight boxer, or tennis champion.

But it's completely different for an actor. Why? Because the re-quirements for acting have nothing to do with strength, speed, or the ability to hit a ball. What separates the good actors from the great ones is their depth of feelings, emotions and experience. Love; lust; laughter; tragedy; fear; pain; anxiety; passion; terror – these are all things that a great actor might have to convincingly portray. It stands to reason that the more intensely you've experienced these things in real life, the easier it will be for you to show them in front of a camera.

Lee Marvin was one of my favorite actors. I always loved the way he played tough, hard drinking, no bullshit kind-of-guys. With his hound dog expression, relaxed posture and gravelly voice, he was utterly convincing in those kind of roles.

But the truth is, none of that was an act. Lee Marvin didn't just play tough guys – he *was* a tough guy. Marvin was a sniper with the U.S. Marines during W.W.II, and was wounded by a Japanese machine gun in the invasion of Saipan. The rest of his platoon was nearly wiped out. That experience, among others, went into making him the kind of man he was. It also made him the actor he was.

Imagine if Lee Marvin had never had all those life experiences. What if he had spent all of his time sheltered in a classroom studying acting instead? Could he have ever played Major John Reisman in *The Dirty Dozen*, or Kid Sheleen in *Cat Ballou*? Do you think he would have ever had an acting career at all?

I don't. In fact, I'm sure he wouldn't have. Marvin got his start in Hollywood by portraying soldiers in war movies. It was his real-life experience in the U.S. Marines that convinced producers he could do it convincingly on the screen, not his acting resume. He barely had an acting resume.

Lee Marvin's story is not unique. Flip back to the "It's the Opposite" chapter and look over all those quotes from the famous movie stars again. Do you get the feeling that any of them ever made acting the most important thing in their lives?

If you read the biographies of great actors, you will find that nearly all had full, fascinating, and in many cases, tumultuous lives. The general public assumes they led interesting lives because they were rich and famous. In fact, I think it was really the other way around; they were rich and famous in large part because they led interesting lives.

Acting mirrors life. If you want to portray it convincingly, you have got to get out there and experience it first-hand. Books won't cut it. Reading is great for lots of things, but it's no substitute for real life experiences. Neither is a classroom. Pack plenty of adventure and romance into your real life, and you probably won't have to worry about taking a class to recover your lost, childhood emotions. You'll be experiencing new ones all the time. Not only is that more effective, it's a hell of a lot more fun.

When all is said and done, maybe that's the best thing about acting. This is a profession that actually *encourages* us to better ourselves and live fuller lives. Outside interests are a distraction in most careers. Not this one. Hobbies, adventures, romance, thrills, danger – it sounds like a cheesy movie trailer from the 1950's, but it's true. Anything you can do to experience life, educate your mind or in any way develop yourself as a human being is bound to make you a better actor.

Some professions force their employees into moral dilemmas and questionable ethics; ours demands that we remain honest and true to ourselves. We have plenty of incentive to stay healthy, look our best and develop our self-confidence. At the same time, we have good reasons to remain humble and guard against becoming self-obsessed. Now, on top of all of those good things, I am also encouraging you to travel and take vacations whenever you can. Can it get any better than that?

FINAL THOUGHTS

"It has been my philosophy of life that difficulties vanish when faced boldly."
- Isaac Asimov

"If I have any genius, it is a genius for living."
- Errol Flynn

Despite its many advantages, an acting career isn't for everybody. After a while, you may decide that it isn't for you. There's nothing wrong with that. In fact, I would consider such an admission to be a positive thing. At least you can check "acting" off your list. When you do, you are one step closer to finding out what you are cutout to be, and that is a step in the right direction.

My hope is that this book inspires you to pursue a career that you enjoy, which in turn allows you to live a better life. I think the biggest mistake any of us can make is to choose a career based purely on the money. Do yourself a favor and forget about the money, at least for now – this is your life we're talking about. Is it really worth spending your life doing something that bores you, or stresses you out, simply for the cash? How much cash is your life worth?

Regardless of what kind of car, house or fancy item you buy, the warm and fuzzy feeling that it gives you will rarely last longer than a couple of weeks. Two weeks of happiness – that's essentially what your stress and hard work has purchased. And as soon as that honeymoon is over, your new toy turns into one more thing for you to clean, maintain and/or worry about. Then what do you do? Run out and buy something else, of course...

If you think about it, grinding your life away in a job you hate, so that you can go out and buy stuff you don't need, isn't much more than self-imposed slavery. When you were a kid dreaming about what you wanted to be when you grew up, I'm guessing that's not what you had in mind.

To avoid such a dismal scenario, it's important that you get on the right track as soon as possible. The good news is that you have already cleared the first hurdle. By reading this book, you have taken time out of your life to explore an occupation that interests you. That is a *huge* step in the right direction.

Every actor would love to be able to work consistently, unfortunately there are only so many roles to go around. That's one of the harsh realities of this business. But failing to make it as an actor doesn't have to mean failure. There are other possibilities.

Maybe you should make your own career path. YouTube will help you do it. As I write this, YouTube has just held their first-ever "Creator Camp" in New York. Through their "NextUp" program, viewers voted for 25 grassroots content creators to receive $35,000, as well as expert training in everything from marketing their brand to lighting their own scenes. Twenty-one year-old Bryan Odell was one of the attendees. He recently hit 50,000 subscribers for his channel, which focuses on the music-scene. He used his modest success on YouTube to move out of the basement of his parents' home in Nebraska. He's already interviewed the likes of Rob Zombie, Korn, and Slipknot. His ultimate mission? "To be the Ryan Seacrest of YouTube." He's on his way...

Fifty-three year-old Emily Kim was another attendee. Three years ago, she was a full-time domestic violence counselor in New York.

Then, for fun, she started uploading videos of herself cooking. Now she has her own cooking channel on YouTube, with 41,000 subscribers tuning in from around the world to watch her prepare either traditional Korean dishes, or her own inventions.

We are rapidly approaching a point in time when every human being on the planet will have access to either a television, computer screen or smart phone. In such a world, the demand for articulate individuals who can speak and carry themselves well in front of a camera continues to grow. The options for you are almost boundless – assuming you have something to say or do. But what if you don't?

Have you considered print? A lot of regional talent agencies handle print work. You don't have to look like a supermodel in order to do it, either. Corporations need print models for magazine ads, posters, flyers, packaging labels and websites. They often want pleasant looking "real people" and photographers love to hire models with an acting background. All you need to get started is your headshot, but eventually you will want to put together a "Comp Card" (also called a "Zed Card"). You can do a search for those terms online to find good examples.

Suppose you are good at speaking and reading, but you just don't seem to be photogenic enough for the camera? In that case, maybe you have a future in voice overs? Voice-over artists are used in every facet of the entertainment, advertising and business world today. Film, television, video games, books-on-tape, commercials and industrials all need quality voices. Everybody loves doing voice-overs because they don't take a lot of time, the money is great and you get to dress comfortably. They are also a lot of fun.

Over the years, my voice work has steadily grown to the point where it now accounts for a substantial percentage of my income. I even have a small recording studio in my basement which allows me to do voice-overs in my underwear, should the mood strike me (have no fear, it rarely does). These days, with the advent of ISDN and high-speed cable, most voice actors operate out of their own homes. It makes working just about as convenient as it could ever be.

It used to be that news anchors had to start out as beat reporters. Now, with the advent of cable television, local, and twenty-four hour news channels such as CNN, CNBC, FOX, MSN and others, that's no longer the case. While it's helpful to have a background in reporting, in the end, it is your skill with a TelePrompTer and how engaging you are in front of the camera that will set you apart from the rest and perhaps determine if you have what it takes to be an anchor. Who knows? Maybe you have a future in the news?

Keep an open mind, and don't discount anything. You never know where it might lead. I sincerely doubt any actor starts out dreaming of becoming a game show host. Peter Marshall certainly didn't. By 1966, he had already landed several small film roles when an opportunity arose for him to host *"The Hollywood Squares"*. Marshall didn't want to do it. He was insulted. He told his agent he was a serious actor. His agent said "Fine. Then act like a game show host". It was tough to argue with that.

Marshall hosted 703 episodes of "The Hollywood Squares" between 1966 and 1982. The show was an enormous success and it proved to be a launching pad for him, making him both rich and famous. For three decades he appeared on nearly every major show on TV. Look him up on www.imdb.com. Today, he has a resume that most actors would kill for.

Oprah Winfrey abandoned her acting career in order to become a TV talk show host. That worked out pretty well for her. Ronald Reagan started out as an actor before turning to politics, and he wound up as President of the United States. Later, he famously announced that he didn't know how anyone could become President *without* being an actor. Actors often do well in politics. The skill sets are almost identical; including mastery of the TelePrompTer.

Whatever path you take and wherever it leads you, I hope this book has helped to open your mind to the world of acting, and perhaps help inspire you to approach your career in a slightly different way. Acting has been a wonderful profession for me, and I would love nothing more than for it to be as good or better to you. If it proves not to be your destiny, then I hope that you are inspired to search for your true calling, and that you achieve the fulfillment and happiness you desire.

With an open mind, a solid work ethic, and the right attitude, there really is no telling how high and far you will go. With luck, perhaps one day I will have an opportunity to read your story. I hope so.

Have fun, do good work, and enjoy the ride!

Suggested Reading

An Actor's Work

By Konstantin Stanislavski (Translated and edited by Jean Benedetti)

The updated translation of Stanislavski's ground-breaking and hugely influential work; this volume contains writing previously published in two separate volumes (*An Actor Prepares*; *Building a Character*) and combines them into one book. I recommend this edition over the others because it is easier to read and preserves Stanislavski's terrific sense of humor. Should be required reading for any actor.

Audition: Everything an Actor Needs to Know to Get the Part

By Michael Shurtleff and Bob Fosse

Valuable insights on auditioning from a former casting director who knows what he's talking about. Michael Shurtleff has worked with some of the biggest names in the business. Based on his many years of experience, he identifies the elements that great actors consistently bring to their auditions, and breaks these down into twelve distinct "guideposts" which you can easily apply to your own work. Auditions will play a major factor in your career, so this is another book that I highly recommend.

Acting for the Camera

By Tony Barr

This goes into greater detail about the technical aspects of working in front of a camera than I have been able to cover here. Worth reading and using as a reference guide until you know your way around a set.

The 4-Hour Workweek

By Timothy Ferris

Not directly related to acting, but it does deal with many aspects that could benefit your acting career. Lots of info on how to set up an automated business online, free-up your time, and escape the corporate grind so that you can focus on doing the things that excite and interest you. Motivational and inspiring.

How to Master the Art of Selling

By Tom Hopkins

The original edition is pretty outdated now, so try to find the revised and updated version if you can. This is the bible of sales books and a must-read for anyone who wants to maximize their chances of having a successful acting career.

ACKNOWLEDGEMENTS

There are many people to whom I owe a huge debt of gratitude for making this book possible. First and foremost, I must thank Andrea Barbian; not only for the many long hours which she spent proofreading and editing, but for remaining my dear friend and companion these many years. Andrea, we have been down quite a road together. Through good times and bad, your honesty, loyalty and intelligence have always shone through. I never met anyone with a bigger heart; or anyone who was quicker to laugh and forgive. You amaze me.

Thanks to my longtime agent and close friend Mystie Buice. Mystie, your qualities as an agent are only surpassed by your qualities as a human being. The value that I place upon your advice and friendship is beyond calculation. Thanks for taking the time out of your crazy schedule to proof-read the chapter on agents, as well as your words of wisdom.

To Wilbur Fitzgerald; actor, drinking buddy and (on occasion) informal legal advisor - thanks for your help in ensuring that my facts and figures were up-to-snuff in the chapter on unions. And thanks too for always being there whenever I have needed your help for anything. Here's a heads-up: If I ever wake up in the county jail at 3 am - you're the poor S.O.B. who's going to get a phone call. I consider myself proud and fortunate to have you as a friend.

Thanks also to Crystal Carson. Crystal is quite simply the best acting teacher that I have ever encountered. Much of the advice I give regarding auditioning for film and television came as a direct result of studying with her. However, that is just a fraction of what she has to offer. Razor sharp insight, energy, experience and dedication to her students are what set her apart from so many others. Crystal has taught in Los Angeles for the past 19 years and her client list includes major stars and household names, but she frequently travels throughout the United States in order to teach and coach in the regional markets. If you are serious about acting and ever have the opportunity to study with her, do it. You won't regret it. Check out www. crystalcarson.com for more information.

If not for Kathryn Carney, this book would probably never have been written in the first place. Kathryn and I started acting about the same time and have remained good friends ever since. Kathryn exudes positive-energy, and it is infectious. I can't begin to count the times she has lit a fire under my backside and gotten me moving. These days, she's a little tough to get a hold of. If she isn't in front of the camera, she's usually behind it. When not producing her own television shows, she tends to gravitate to secluded beaches on the other side of the world. Kathryn, I can't thank you enough for all of the help, advice and adventures; as well as for being my personal marketing guru, free of charge.

There are many others who have played a part in making this possible. Thanks to Jodi Marks for allowing me to share the harrowing story of her first acting experience, both in real-time and in the book. Thanks to Jonathan Greenhill for helping me to get the book into a finalized form. Thanks to my good buddies Brian Nelsen, Drew Edwards, Dave Adam, Lawayne Bontrager, John Ashbaugh and others for offering their own help and advice whenever possible.

Thanks to Judson Vaughn for introducing me to the world of acting. Remember when I was flat on my back and Ann suggested that I call a friend of a friend? Judson was the guy I called. Judson had spent about ten years trying to make it as an actor in Los Angeles before finally giving up and moving back east. He had planned to retire from acting altogether, but as is so often the case, moving out of L.A. turned out to be the spark that ignited his career. I was incredibly fortunate in that my first acting instructor also happened to be a full-time actor who understood the business well. Among other things, Judson taught me the importance of sales in acting, and why it is vital to raise your rates as soon as possible. I shall be forever grateful to him for getting me on the right path early.

Finally, I want to thank the two people to whom this book is dedicated; my mom and dad. I think if I had had the chance to hand-pick my own parents, I could not have chosen better. Thanks for your love, guidance, and example; for encouraging me to march to the beat of my own drum, and for insisting that I stand on my own two feet whenever problems arose - even when every parental instinct must have urged you to rush in and save me. Looking back now, I wouldn't have had it any other way. I love you both, and owe you everything.

INDEX

13974719R00173

Made in the USA
Lexington, KY
01 March 2012